Praise for

In *The Voices We Carry*, J. S. Park shape so much of the way we move through the world, without our even knowing it. In identifying those voices and giving us examples from his own personal and professional life, examples that are often astonishingly honest, he becomes a sturdy guide and trusted friend in the journey. We may all carry these voices, but we don't need to carry them alone. *The Voices We Carry* bursts with compassion and wisdom. This book is a gift.

KERRY EGAN
Author of *On Living*

J. S. has written a personal narrative that gives a "voice" to the "voices" we all encounter—those internal dialogues we fight and embrace that cycle through messages of rejection and belonging. Through his experience as a chaplain and the vulnerability of his personal experiences growing up, J. S. weaves a message of hope that we have the power to identify, confront, and ultimately transform our personal dialogue when we choose to step into and embrace the authenticity of our unique voice.

DEBORAH GORTON
Licensed clinical psychologist, author, Gary D. Chapman Chair of Marriage, Family Ministry, and Therapy at Moody Theological Seminary

The exposing honesty of triumph over human failure, especially in J. S. Park, is mind remedying. Reading J. S.'s heart and faith throughout *The Voices We Carry* gives courage to listen to, decipher, face, and positively redirect the voices that live inside our humanness, our minds, and our hearts. Helping us to become overcomers in order to help others to overcome is a beautiful and generous gift from God. *The Voices We Carry* challenges us to recognize we all are a part of God's gift, through the presence of the Holy Spirit guiding us, by the power of Jesus' love made complete in us.

BELINDA W. WOMACK
Internationally renowned gospel and jazz artist

We all carry darkness. And we all carry light. Learning to let our light illuminate our darkness and expose the most vulnerable, flawed, broken parts of ourselves frees us to become the unashamedly human, miraculously divine image-bearers we were created to be and, in the process, opens our hearts to the other vulnerable, flawed, broken humans we encounter every day. That is the healing message of *The Voices We Carry*. With practical steps interspersed with personal stories in the powerful voice of a hospital chaplain, *The Voices We Carry* is more than a self-help book or a memoir. It is a revelation of what it means to be human in an often inhumane world. It is an invitation to be fully and fiercely and authentically human despite, or even because of, our frailty and failings and to reach out to each other, again and again, in the face of the sometimes insurmountable grief of life and love and loss on this gorgeous old planet we share.

L. R. KNOST
Author of *InHumanity: Letters from the Trenches* and *Two Thousand Kisses a Day: Gentle Parenting Through the Ages and Stages*

J. S. Park gives us all an incredible gift in *The Voices We Carry*: the chance to be known and seen by a chaplain, perhaps even long before we find ourselves at the end of our days. His writing is singular and unique: he is a poet, a theologian, and a guide to the inner worlds we expend momentous energy hiding from the rest of the world. I will be reading this book over and over again: it exposes and it heals, all at the same time pointing us toward the divine voice of love we are so desperately craving.

D. L. MAYFIELD
Author of *The Myth of the American Dream: Reflections on Affluence, Autonomy, Safety, and Power*

J. S. Park has masterfully captured a God-honoring expression of giving voice to the unheard souls seeking hope in the midst of trauma, grief, and faith.

MORRIS HINTZMAN
Developing Founder and Former President of Metropolitan Ministries, Tampa, FL

the voices we carry

FINDING YOUR ONE
TRUE VOICE IN A WORLD
OF CLAMOR AND NOISE

j. s. park

NORTHFIELD PUBLISHING
CHICAGO

All Scripture quotations, unless otherwise indicated, are taken from the Holy Bible, New International Version®, NIV®. Copyright © 1973, 1978, 1984, 2011 by Biblica, Inc.™ Used by permission of Zondervan. All rights reserved worldwide. www.zondervan.com. The "NIV" and "New International Version" are trademarks registered in the United States Patent and Trademark Office by Biblica, Inc.™

Scripture quotations marked KJV are taken from the King James Version.

All emphasis in Scripture has been added.

Brief sections in chapters 4 and 12 were included in previously published posts on the author's blog: jsparkblog.com.

Names and details in some stories have been changed to protect the privacy of individuals.

Published in association with the literary agency of Legacy, LLC, 501 N. Orlando Avenue, Suite #313-348, Winter Park, FL 32789.

Edited by Amanda Cleary Eastep
Interior and cover design: Erik M. Peterson

All websites and phone numbers listed herein are accurate at the time of publication but may change in the future or cease to exist. The listing of website references and resources does not imply publisher endorsement of the site's entire contents. Groups and organizations are listed for informational purposes, and listing does not imply publisher endorsement of their activities.

Library of Congress Cataloging-in-Publication Data

Names: Park, J. S. (Hospital chaplain), author.
Title: The voices we carry : finding your one true voice in a world of
    clamor and noise / J.S. Park.
Description: Chicago : Northfield Publishing, [2020] | Includes
    bibliographical references. | Summary: "Quiet the Noise in Your
    Headspace and Find Your One, True Voice During hospital chaplaincy
    training, J. S. Park began to see patterns in his own life and the lives
    of patients he met. Often they understood the problem, maybe, like him,
    they could even point to the root causes, but they still felt stuck. So
    he developed the Voices Model to help people find their one, true voice.
    It explores the false voices we listen to, four inner voices
    (self-condemning, self-exalting, condemning others, and exalting
    others), and four outer voices (guilt, family dynamics, grief, and
    trauma). Through it you'll learn how to identify these unhelpful voices
    and successfully kick them out of your headspace. Filled with
    first-person narrative stories, and psychological, spiritual, and
    clinical insights, The Voices We Carry is an enjoyable, disarming, and
    important read. For anyone who wants to grow but isn't quite sure how to
    move forward, this book is for you"-- Provided by publisher.
Identifiers: LCCN 2019055264 (print) | LCCN 2019055265 (ebook) | ISBN
    9780802419897 (paperback) | ISBN 9780802498816 (ebook)
Subjects: LCSH: Self-talk. | Self-perception. | Self-actualization
    (Psychology) | Self-realization.
Classification: LCC BF697.5.S47 P37 2020 (print) | LCC BF697.5.S47
    (ebook) | DDC 158.1--dc23
LC record available at https://lccn.loc.gov/2019055264
LC ebook record available at https://lccn.loc.gov/2019055265

We hope you enjoy this book from Northfield Publishing. Our goal is to provide high-quality, thought-provoking books and products that connect truth to your real needs and challenges. For more information on other books and products that will help you with all your important relationships, go to: www.moodypublishers.com or write to:

Northfield Publishing
820 N. LaSalle Boulevard
Chicago, IL 60610

1 3 5 7 9 10 8 6 4 2

Printed in the United States of America

To Juliette,
my steady whisper,
my loudest advocate.
I couldn't and wouldn't do this without you.

To John E.,
you were a voice of joy and good cheer,
a voice I will always miss,
a voice I will always hear.

To my brother and my parents,
you taught me to survive,
and every day, you inspire.

Author's Note

Names and details of some stories have been changed to protect the privacy of individuals. Many of the persons in this book are composites. This was done by a combination of addition, subtraction, and conflation. The spirit of the stories remains intact.

Many studies are cited throughout the book. Please note that the field of psychology continues to struggle with a methodology problem called the Replication Crisis, in which studies are not always reliably replicated. However, it's possible that differing results are highlighting previously unknown variables, which is helping to expand knowledge rather than contradicting previous results.

The following pages contain suggestions but not medical advice. For the latter, please consult your physician.

Contents

PART 3: Finding Your Voice

Foreword

I cannot remember exactly what my Google search words were, but they were probably "insignificance," "heartbroken," "faith," and "anxiety." I might have also typed "non-judgmental advice from pastor who is not afraid of hard questions." I found myself reading Joon's [J. S.] posts earnestly, and then poring through his site. I was surprised at how refreshingly honest, gracious, and thoughtful he was in addressing difficult issues that I was too afraid to share. His posts helped me realize I was not alone in my struggles.

I emailed Joon to tell him how much his posts spoke to me. He replied, and we became friends through Facebook Messenger and Instagram DMs. We finally met in person last year in LA. He was there to interview a few people for this book, and those few people included me! Now I was nervous. I was comfortable hiding behind a screen, chatting and reading his posts, but meeting in person was different! What if he turned out to be totally different from his online persona? What if he found me awkward?

When I met Joon, I knew I fretted for nothing. He was warm, friendly, and approachable. We talked for many hours that day. Over our Mexican lunch and then over our afternoon coffee, we talked about fear and creativity, about shrinking back from negative social media comments, about his chaplaincy work and my recent trip to a refugee school in Lebanon, about his martial arts background, and about the dreaded topic of anxiety and depression—conversation topics that make me very embarrassed, somewhat ashamed, and uncomfortable. It's so hard to admit to the ugly and controlling thoughts in my head, but it was easy talking to Joon about this. It was clear that Joon loves people. He was humble, sensitive, and kind. I knew I could trust him as I opened up about my thoughts and feelings. His friendship is one without judgment or pretense. I felt accepted as I was.

I know this book will make you feel the same.

This book addresses self-doubt, people-pleasing, trauma and grief, and finding your voice in the sea of voices in our heads. Joon shares his joy and pain as a hospital chaplain and his relationship with family. Through poignant self-reflection, he points out that this book is about every one of us and not a book for us to point fingers at others. Joon speaks with genuine concern for people through a combination of personal experience, faith, and research on mental health. *The Voices We Carry* is about how all of us have voices in our heads that can control us but that we can overcome.

It is easy to cave in to lies and let them become our reality. Joon has helped me learn that it is okay to admit pain. In this book, he will walk you through your pain and lead you, through empathy and compassion, to finding a clear voice.

Joon's greatest gift is his heart for those of us who struggle. He both sits and walks with people through their challenges. Joon told me once about how he heard that "everyone is thankful, but the difference is expressing that gratitude." I am so grateful, Joon, for your friendship and for this book.

RED HONG YI
Visual Artist

You Are World of Voices

My assumption is
that the story of any one of us
is in some measure
the story of us all.

—FREDERICK BUECHNER, *THE SACRED JOURNEY:*
A MEMOIR OF EARLY DAYS[1]

THE SERIOUS STUFF

I'm a hospital chaplain and part of my job is to listen. All day long, I hear voices.

As I've listened to patients, I've learned that I'm not just hearing their voice, but I'm hearing all the voices they carry.

Here's what I mean. I visit a patient who tells me, "I have to get out of here. I have to get back to work. If I stop working, I don't matter."

"Don't matter?"

"Yeah, chap. I got this loop in my head. You know the one? It says, 'You stop working, then *you stop existing.*'"

I got that. A whole lot.

In a rare moment of pushback, I asked, "Says who? Who told you that?"

The patient opens his mouth. He turns his ear, like he's tuning his antenna.

"It sounds like the voice of my father," he says. "And my boss. My trauma, too, I guess. But chap, mostly that voice is me."

Every patient—every one of us, really—is living that way. We are a world of voices that tell us who we are, how to move, and how to be. Sometimes they're barely audible, and they whisper in our guts all the time, almost out of earshot. But they're there, making all kinds of suggestions.

The voice can be a message as simple as,

They'll find out you're no good, or,

Keep them happy or they'll leave, or,

Only you can save these people.

These voices can come from an entangled knot of our fathers and failures and the things that happened to us. They come from trauma and triumphs, our hometown rumors, the thing our spouse or child said before we went out the door, the teacher in fifth grade who dismissed our questions, the comments online, the hashtags and headlines, advice and opinions and blogs, the family dinner table. The voices also emerge from inside: our self-doubt, our pride, our need to be liked, our need to fix the universe. Without confronting these things, they can keep us stuck in an automated theater, a real Sisyphus-type puppet show.

Over and over, I have seen hundreds of patients, many near death, so overwhelmed by their voices that they can hardly make their own choices. They were at the mercy of wildly disparate shouts, pulling them through a dissonant and contradictory fog.

The same was true for me. When I walked into a patient's room, I did not walk in alone. I carried scars and motives and echoes. Like a lot of my patients, I was a real mixed-up guy, suffocating on an inner monologue that ascribed my value, a confusing script of all the things I thought I was supposed to be.

But as I journeyed with my patients, I noticed another common theme. I met patients who, with a little help, had managed their own voices. I don't mean they just turned the volume down; I mean they entered into dialogue with themselves. They engaged with their trauma, their family of origin, and their rehearsed prescriptions for self-worth, and they turned these voices to their own advantage. They did not just overcome their voices, but found a profound and gentle strength from them. I had seen it happen in my patients and in my fellow chaplains. I had seen it in myself.

When the patient who told me, *If I stop working, I don't matter,* could finally name his voices—his father, his trauma, himself— he started the path to unravel the loop in his head. He found peace, not just in the noise, but from the noise. Nobody had told him it was possible, but it is.

As a hospital chaplain, I finally learned to listen. Not just to others' voices, but to all the stuff swirling in my own head. I listened, and in these voices I found clues to becoming whole.

— — —

This is serious stuff. Our voices have unimaginable power. All of us give over a certain amount of control to them. Not on purpose, but we may let them falsely accuse, fabricate conspiracies, confuse us, and steer us. If you've ever had negative self-talk, someone's harsh words ringing between your ears, a late-night loop in your head, then you know what I mean. The good news is that all these voices can be redeemed. Even befriended. After all, many of our voices are a way to gain worth and structure—even as their methods steal the very things they meant to sustain. If we unscramble these distorted, garbled signals—that is, if we give our voices a listen and ask some questions—then we find in many ways they're not a script to be trashed, but a gift to unwrap. They may prevent us from being our truest selves, but they also may open the way to get there.

We find that while we carry voices, they can carry us too.

One of the purposes of this book is to identify the voices that have shaped who we are and how we see others and ourselves. I'll talk about how these voices may have harmed us and how to move through them. I'll talk about how these voices may be broken and misinformed, but that they can be restored and made good.

EAR TO THE GROUND

Here's where we're going.

As a hospital chaplain, I've learned invaluable lessons at the edge of life and death from some of the best people I've ever met: my patients. In the pages that follow, I will share moments from that experience and draw from the insight I've gained to help answer these important questions for you:

What voices are controlling me? How much have I been swayed and deceived by them? Where do they come from and what's their

14

goal? How are they affecting others around me? What are these voices really saying? How do I manage them? Reject them? What does it look like to redeem them?

We'll be talking about four internal voices and four external ones. The internal voices are the ones that harshly evaluate everybody, including ourselves. If you've ever been hard on yourself or on somebody else, you've experienced them plenty. The external voices are influences that intrude from the outside-in, and they're usually painful. They sort of fall in your lap, from situations beyond your control, like grief or your family of origin. Those external voices may seem like they're not all worthwhile, but we'll find there's a way to glean good from them. We'll also talk about sifting through the clamor and noise so we can solidify our own voice, as we do the same for those who have no voice of their own.

MORE THAN YOU THINK

Before we go on, I have to tell you about this study. You may be tired of studies, but this one's really something.

I was reading about a new therapy program for people with verbal auditory hallucinations.[2] Over half of people with schizophrenia suffer from this. The voices in their heads are awful and unrelenting, and a quarter of those with psychotic symptoms don't get better with medicine or therapy.

Researchers gathered some patients with schizophrenia, and for each one, created an audio-visual avatar of their hallucination called the "persecutor." The researchers even matched the pitch and tone of the avatar to the hallucinations. The avatars were controlled by a therapist, and at first the avatars would act like they always did, hostile and dominating, but the avatar would slowly yield to the patient over time.

It worked. As the therapists adjusted the avatars, each patient gained power over them, and eventually the voices in their head also reduced in both frequency and severity. For some patients, *the harmful voices completely stopped.* The avatar program was repeated again with a bigger group. After twelve weeks, over 80 percent of the patients reported the same effects.[3]

This study is an extreme example, but every one of us has experienced the relentless bombardment of voices. We may need medicine or therapy or specially customized avatars to get through them. But the big idea is that we're already more powerful than we believe. We're more than the stuff in our heads.

When your voices keep talking, you can talk back.

I Don't Know How Much I Didn't Know

They all carried ghosts.
—TIM O'BRIEN, *THE THINGS THEY CARRIED*[1]

MY VOICES: YOU ARE (NOT) AN ACCIDENT

These are some of the voices I used to wrestle with.

Do you hear them, too?

You are an accident.

I was born an accident, out of wedlock, to two hesitant immigrant parents who didn't know if they would keep me or stay together. The one before me was aborted.

I found out about the "accident" around my twelfth birthday, and for a while I walked around like some kind of superimposed hologram, a ghost in debt. I apologized a lot, bowing my head in short little bobs, always sorry about everything. You might have seen a guy figuring out how to get through a crowded hallway without bumping into everyone and making a mess of the world: you have seen me. I moved with the finesse of rolling a boulder up a stream. My head-space was always haunted by second-guessing, and I had nightmares of jumpstarting the butterfly effect and ripping a hole in the sky. Real plague-type stuff. It was a crazy thing, walking around with a drag of cosmic displacement—a life on loan—wondering about parallel timelines. My every good deed was a deposit in a black hole; my every bad deed was a confirmation that I should not be around so much. I was possessed by a phantom of deficit.

The story I believed about myself was: *You're an interruption to the order of things.*

That was the voice in my head.

You are sick and something is wrong with you.

My parents married because of me. They divorced on my fourteenth birthday. It was probably because of all the cheating, but those were symptoms, like they say, of deeper stuff. I was an extremely sick child—chronic bronchitis, asthma attacks, bouts of vertigo, allergies to fruit, dairy, and dogs, and there was the one time that penicillin nearly killed me—and for a year I took a daily dose of medicine through a nebulizer. In my culture, there's a belief that disease comes from some rotten place in your soul. I was told my constant illness was a symptom of something, a stench rising from bad soil.

My uncle had schizophrenia and suffered from hallucinations. He always thought someone was after him. I mean it, like really chasing him. He put red beans in his ears to stop all the radio signals, and occasionally he hopped on his bicycle with nothing but a backpack full of underwear and would ride from Florida to California. He did this once or twice a year. I don't think it helped. My grandmother was a fully practicing Shintoist. I still couldn't tell you what it's all about. She chanted these intense Shinto prayers for hours in a closet by incense, and I decided early on I was an atheist. My grandmother developed dementia. I remember her cooking for me and my brother as my parents lived their separate lives, the dinners becoming more and more bizarre, my grandmother shouting at spirits in the kitchen as smoke rose from the pots and pans.

You are not welcome.

My father was a second lieutenant in the Vietnam War and served alongside the US. He was captured by the Viet Cong in an assault called the Tet Offensive—he was blindfolded, bound, and transported barefoot to a prison camp. He was a POW for years. He escaped, just barely, by killing the guards. He still gets phone calls from families looking for their fathers who were captured. He moved to New York with fifty dollars in his wallet, as he tells it, and through his charm and investors, opened a martial arts dojo. He moved to Florida and opened another. I was around for the one in Florida.

One summer, someone spray-painted a swastika on the front wall of the dojo. My father painted over it, but I could still see the red crosshairs under the paint, throbbing like an angry scar in the summer sun. Another time we got a message on our answering machine, maybe the same Nazi artists, and they left a ten-minute message making fun of my father's accent. I remember seeing my father play it several times, staring quietly out a window. He noticed me and turned it off. "Just boys playing a joke," he said. He knew as well as I did that the voices were not from boys.

You cannot lose.

My parents worked a lot, my father at his martial arts dojo and my mother working nights at her laundromat and days at her grocery store. We fit the stereotypes neatly. I'd watch my mother leave at midnight, come home before the sun rose, sleep an hour, then get right back to work. The TV was always on. Somehow we still made it to dinner together every night on the floor of my parents' bedroom at a raggedy wooden table. We watched whatever my father wanted to, which was boxing mostly, or an action movie. If we had a good week, we'd go to Stacey's Buffet in the next town over, and my father always said the same thing while holding up a fried chicken leg: *This is when I feel like I'm in America.*

We were poor, but I didn't know what that meant. We lived in what I'm sure was the projects. I loved our little place, a huddle from the world, stains and all. My brother and I chased the cockroaches that visited us from the walls and we threw them at each other and I'd land the most and win. When I was seven, I got in a fight with a single mother from the projects, and I lost. To my credit, she started it. My mother scolded me later, telling me, *Always fight to win.*

My parents lost the laundromat and grocery store, but the dojo took off. At twelve years old, when I found out I was a mistake, we moved into a three-story house with twenty-two windows out front. But my parents' marriage went sideways. It was probably the money. They argued about everything in an instant. I could feel the heat building in the room like a copper electric taste in my mouth, and then one wrong word set the world on fire. Lamps were thrown, wardrobes tossed, windows broken. My mother sliced open my father with her middle fingernail from his elbow to his wrist. They punched each other in the face, with wild, full-swing haymakers. The police visited with some regularity. I missed the roaches.

You are not one of us.

In sixth grade, I had allergies, glasses, braces, and a stutter all at the same time. That was social death. Two girls passed a note to me one time in homeroom, and I got pretty excited. I mean a note from two girls. On one side the note said *Ugly Pass,* and on the other it said, *You can show your ugly face in school today.*

I sat alone at lunch in the cafeteria. One guy took a swing at me because "your dad fought my dad in the war." Another time I guess I was sitting too close to this table of acceptable people, and they threw French fries at my head. The fries were drenched in ketchup, naturally.

The popular sixth graders, about five of them, one time cornered Victor, a smart Jewish kid with glasses, in the locker room and beat him unconscious. I saw Victor's face later; the violence was startling. The guys who beat him up were suspended from school for a week and Victor ended up switching schools.

A few weeks later, the popular kids told me that Landra liked me. Landra, to me, was the prettiest girl in the entire school. She was the leader of the popular girls. For days, the guys took turns telling me, *Landra likes you, man, she thinks you're cute, she likes Chinese guys, she thinks you're funny, you should ask her out.*

I didn't believe it at first, thinking this was some kind of Victor locker room situation. But I mean, the guys were actually nice to me, and that was all they ever talked about: *She likes you, seriously, you and her could go steady.*

The power of their voices got to me.

So at lunch in the cafeteria, I approached Landra as she left the lunch line. I remember what she was wearing that day: a blue dress imprinted with white flowers, a black headband, a lace choker. Believe me, I was sweating from everywhere. I was sort of giddy and dizzy and nauseated at the same time. But I had it on good intel that this would go really well. This was my chance to turn my sorry life around.

I tapped Landra on the shoulder. She smiled at me.

I knew it, I thought. *She really does like me.*

I said, "I like you . . . too?"

To her credit, she wasn't mean to me or anything. She put her hand on my shoulder and gave me this sad sort of smile. I still think about that sometimes, the way people can be kind in a hard situation.

She said, "No." And she walked away. I can still see her dress, the way her headband fit her hair.

At one side of the cafeteria, where the popular guys sat, I heard them laughing. They were muffled at first, but soon busted out in a roar, holding their sides and pointing at me and slapping the table. I ran out the back of the cafeteria and went to the restroom and I sat on a toilet and cried. I didn't come out of the restroom for the rest of the day.

I ended up switching schools too.

You don't have what it takes.

My father took me to this audition for a TV show on Nickelodeon when I was about six years old. I mean, imagine that. At six, that's a really big deal. I was part of this pre-selected group of *potential stars* because I had shown up in a newspaper article about my father's dojo, and my father knew some hotshot studio executive and showed off my face from the metro section—and so began my career in show business.

It ended pretty quickly.

I went with my father in his beat-up Lincoln Continental to this casting place between a dry cleaners and a pawn shop. The second I walked in, I saw a bunch of other kids with their parents in the waiting room. The kids were practicing with their parents. They were dead serious; it was like a haunted nursery. And they were *good.* Have you ever seen those precocious glassy-eyed kids who act like adults, and it's sort of cute and creepy all at once? This waiting room had all of them. I was still trying to figure out what to do with my arms; these kids were method acting and reciting lines from Othello.

I had questions. *Should I have been practicing? Do I want to do this? Am I wearing pants right now?* I sat down with my father and tried to practice, but I noticed my own voice for the first time and it was really loud in my ears. I expected a certain noise and out came another.

I walked into this room as one kind of kid and sat down a completely different kid. From elated to deflated, in the span of one iambic pentameter.

It was my turn. My father and I walked through a tiny door that revealed half a set: an empty desk, an ottoman, a fern, a couch, a studio light, and a video camera on a tripod. Everything was a teal and burgundy color, which made me want to brush my teeth. The casting director, an impossibly tall guy with a headset and a clipboard, gave me the assignment. I was supposed to jump out from behind the couch and say a catchphrase: *Not in my house!*

Suddenly I was feverish. The casting director looked me up and down and jotted some notes. He looked intensely uninterested. The light was hot, I mean oven hot. I noticed the fern was fake, a sickening greenish plastic, and the ottoman was faded and peeling at the corners. I got behind the couch. It had no backing, just some plywood covered in cobwebs. The floorboards squeaked. I became really aware that my arms were a thing I could control with my brain. My hands felt disconnected from my body, sort of flopping around on their own. The room spun. I wanted to run.

The casting guy said *action*—and I jumped up and yelled my line.

"Not in my house!"

I stood there and looked at the casting guy. The casting guy looked at me. He made a note. A really long note. A couple notes. Then he looked up and said, "You have to put in *more.* Put more into it. Okay? More."

I reset. I was sweating a lot, half from the light and half from myself.

"Not in my *house!*" Reset. "Not in *my* house!" Reset. "Not in my house?"

I never got a call back.

You are Bruce.

In my senior year of high school, this administrator told me about a multicultural festival that would be attended by the entire high school. Hundreds of students, maybe. *Would you like to be a part of that?* he asked. *Would you like to show off your martial arts?* he asked. *Yes,* I said. *Yes, I would.*

I trained. For weeks I ran and kicked and jumped and kicked some more until my legs just about fell off. I put together music on a cassette tape. On the big day, I drove up in my beat-down Toyota Corolla with my uniform and black belt and nunchucks and I froze. I stayed in the car and sobbed these heaving, panicked sobs. Oh man, a big black belt baby. I couldn't do it. No one liked me here, anyway. They would laugh me off the stage with French fries and ugly passes. *You wanted to be one of us, huh? One of us?*

One of my father's students, a middle-aged guy named Dom, had agreed to meet me in the school parking lot to help me out. He volunteered to hold boards and be the *uki,* the fall guy. Dom believed in me, I think. He thought I was all right. He knocked on my car window and it sort of snapped me out of the crying fit. I think he had seen me crying in the car but he didn't say anything.

I grabbed my belt, my nunchucks, my boards, and my cassette tape, and I strode into the high school gymnasium and handed the tape to the DJ. Everyone was there. Hundreds of students. It felt like a million. They didn't look mean or anything; more like surprised, or sorry even. The music queued up, and for a second I was going to run out of the building. I looked at Dom. He looked sort of hopeful and sad and kind all at once, the way you look at a kid who gets picked last for the team but you want him to have a good time. I picked up the chucks and spun them like crazy. I did all my flashy moves. I jumped around and threw all the kicks I had practiced, those hours and hours of kicks in the mirror until my legs had turned to jelly. And the students cheered. *Cheered.* Not the polite kind, but the gasping kind, like can you get a load of this guy?—he's all right. I did more flashy stuff on Dom the *uki*; I threw him left and right and he really sold it. Then I lined up eight football players to crouch on the ground and Dom held a board at the end of the line, and I jumped over all eight football players for a flying side kick finish. When I landed, no one moved for a full two seconds. I thought I had lost them. But the place went wild. Someone yelled *Bruce!*—for Bruce Lee. I was Bruce for the rest of my senior year.

I've seen those high schoolers again, at the mall or a doctor's office or some place, and they silently whisper, *Bruce*. That was my one moment of high school redemption, like the gawky kid who does a cool dance number at prom, except I beat up Dom and jumped over football players.

Everyone should get one of those memories. Not everyone does, I know. I was lucky.

THIS TIME (AND EVERY TIME), IT'S PERSONAL

By the time I entered the hospital chaplaincy program, I found out a sad thing: I wasn't healthy. Despite a few good voices, all those hard ones had done a number on me.

The chaplaincy program wasn't what I expected. I thought we would learn how to counsel patients in their grief. That was a part of it. But to figure out how to counsel grief, we also had to counsel our own. The program was basically one long self-surgery, with a mirror overhead.

The job interview was a big indication of all this. Instead of asking the usual stuff like, "What do you think you'll contribute here?" or "What's your leadership style?", they asked "How did your parents' divorce affect you?" and "How did you feel about your previous boss when he fired you?"

"How did I feel?"

"Yes. Your feelings."

"Oh. Those. My feelings . . . felt bad."

"*Bad* is not a feeling word."

I remember thinking these were *personal questions*. Let's be professional; you can't ask me that.

How did you process your friend's death in college?

What made you want to take your life twelve years ago?

What happened just now when you flinched at that question?

What did you feel?

The interview went on like this for an hour. It was icky and uncomfortable. Like a fork across my gums. They told me they would call me in a month. I thought I had bombed it. Afterward, I drove around for a while, recovering from digging through my old wounds. I had those mad tears. I mean, they asked me about my *life*. A few hours later, they called. Congratulations, they said. You're hired.

"The interview," a supervisor said at orientation, "was only to find out two things: to see if you're teachable and to see if you can lean into your pain."

I laughed a little. I sort of wanted to punch him. But I was afraid they would spend an hour asking me why.

— — —

The whole program was like the interview: we would dig deep, tap a well of stories, then dig some more. Into our *feelings*. It was ridiculous—maybe self-indulgent—but it was revealing.

The entire thing was a six-month internship and a yearlong residency. There were five interns and five residents. We varied in age, gender, race, religion, and background. We called it an arranged marriage. Imagine you get thrown into a rock tumbler and at the other end you hope the friction will make you a gem. That was the idea, anyway.

We'd meet up weekly for a few hours of classes, patient discussions, one-on-one supervisions with the supervisor, topical reflections, and group time. This was hard stuff. Especially the group time, called IPR—Interpersonal Relations—where we dug into each other's stories, called each other out, and put "why we do what we do" under a microscope. Sometimes all of this was harder than visiting the patients. In IPR, with our different ears and eyes and perspectives, we discovered things in ourselves that we never could have on our own.

BEHIND THE CURTAIN: ANOTHER CURTAIN

In chaplaincy, we were tasked to ask ourselves: *What are the stories under our stories? And what's underneath those stories?*

I discovered, slowly and painfully, that the failure to confront all my voices had produced a fractured, nervous, anxious, and self-shaming sort of person. I flopped over quickly at criticism. The slightest feedback would send me into a tailspin of self-loathing. But then I had an ego big enough to see from space. I found out I was more judgmental than I could ever admit, exerting a mental control over the actions of other people who were "lesser" than me. At the same time, I exalted others so much I was always living out their vision for me.

I discovered that I suffered from a contradiction of self-doubt, egotism, bigotry, and people-pleasing. There was no Dr. Jekyll, only Mr. Hyde and Hyde and Hyde. I identified these voices that had burrowed their way in, carving subterranean divots from which they whispered their commands. I found these same voices in hundreds of my patients from all walks of life—and at death. I found them in the other chaplains as we traced our histories together. Mostly I found them in myself. It was in hearing these voices that I really began to *see*.

Really, I shouldn't have been surprised. But I was. Before chaplaincy, I didn't have names for the things I carried with me. Putting a name to them was liberating. Excruciating. Empowering.

— — —

In the Philip Marlowe detective stories, shady characters are always walking into Marlowe's office or bumping into him at the scene of the crime. Marlowe has to figure out fast if they're a crook or a patsy, how they fit into the puzzle, if they can be trusted. In the end, he works with them, turns them in, or both.

In some sense, our brains are their own sort of detective story, complete with a cast of characters we've learned to trust or dismiss. Each character—each voice—has either guided us out of the fog or led us into an alley. A lot of times, we've remained in the limbo of mystery, never finding out who we can trust.

But these voices left unchecked can be harmful. They can subtly direct the course of your life. Your relationships. Your marriage. Your work. Your home.

Take it from me: it's worth the investigation. It's worth chasing all these voices as far as they can go.

— — —

In this book, we'll go through **four internal voices** and **four external voices**.

The four internal voices are *valuations.* They grade others and ourselves; they confer moral judgments. These four voices—self-exaltation, self-condemnation, exalting others, and condemning others—at first appear negative, since they victimize or demonize. But by getting the entire story on these voices, we can instead *humanize* others and ourselves. We find there's a purpose behind each voice, each trying to say something that isn't what it seems.

INTERNAL VOICES MODEL: VALUATIONS

	SELF	OTHERS
EXALTING	**SELF-EXALTATION:** Pride and Self-Justification	**EXALTING OTHERS:** People-Pleasing and Codependency
CONDEMNING	**SELF-CONDEMNATION:** Self-Doubt, Second-Guessing, and Insecurity	**CONDEMNING OTHERS:** Judgment, Resentment, and Controlling Others

The four external voices are *precipitations*. They tend to occur from events and situations outside of us, often things we can't control. They are guilt, trauma, family dynamics, and grief. They don't always have redeeming qualities, but there's a way to face them with poise and skill.

EXTERNAL VOICES MODEL: PRECIPITATIONS

	SELF	OTHERS
PAIN FROM	**GUILT:** What I Did	**FAMILY DYNAMICS:** What I Grew Up With
LOSS FROM	**TRAUMA:** What Was Done to Me	**GRIEF:** What I Lost

Most of the voices I talk about in this book will sound familiar. But some of our voices will have to be dug up, and they might not like it. They might hiss at exposure to light. Some of that's because these voices have been giving orders for a while. They're so comfortable that they've offered a false kind of safety. For example, we may routinely find reasons to belittle ourselves. That feeling of condemnation, then, becomes a cozy and terrible blanket. If we question that voice, it might counter, *But the proof is right there, you messed it up pretty bad, so don't ever try that again.* And so we stay stuck and wrapped up. Other times, we've been taught the wrong way to navigate through these voices: to overpower them, erase them, ignore them. The voices of grief and family dynamics, for example, are supposed to be "let go." Letting go of those voices, we find, is not only impossible, but harmful. They can enrich us, if we negotiate with them.

Exploring some of these voices might be an ugly street fight. Some of this will be challenging. At some point you might get tempted to think, *Oh, I know a guy who does that. I wish that guy could hear this.* And I bet this book would be good for that guy. But really, I'm talking to you. I promise I'm also talking to me and that other guy too. Mainly, though, it's for you. I'm pulling up a chair, eye-to-eye, face-to-face, and with all the grace and hope and love and anticipation in my being. Together we'll find a way through these voices to wholeness. By that, I mean finding the unswayed soul, your truest, most grounded self, moving freely through the clamor and noise.

We'll conclude the book by going through three ways that our voices can be used for good. I'll talk about what it means to uncover lies to find truth worth holding, how to find your own voice amid mixed messages, and how to give a voice to the voiceless. And I'll talk about the one true voice, the one "divine," who has been there all along.

PART 1

Internal Voices

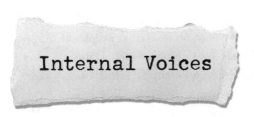

Internal Voices

The first voices we'll deal with are *valuations*—how we grade others and ourselves. They're about the way we lift up and tear down, how we idolize and demonize. Valuations have a moral dimension to them, in that they prescribe worth on a sliding scale. Generally, it doesn't go well.

In a one-on-one supervision during my chaplaincy training, I described my valuations, these competing internal voices. If you're like me, your internal voices fluctuate between dramatic extremes. Imagine overhearing my conversation with Audrey, my training supervisor, as I related my thoughts in a sort of deranged, manic tone:

> When I'm riding high and doing all the things, I start to think
> I'm bigger and better than everybody. I'm climbing the charts
> and climbing over these fools, right? You ever get that rush?
> The surge of euphoria in your bowels? Just me? But then I
> mess up and I'm headfirst in a ditch. The bad kind of fall. I
> mean, floppy arms all sideways and mangled. Somebody
> might close a door on me and then I run around headless
> to answer their whims until I can change their minds. You
> know, the old dilemma: one day I'm awesome, the next day
> I'm throwing away all my mirrors. I ricochet between pride
> and despair like a flip-flop parabola. A single page of my inner
> monologue looks like the worst roller coaster ever. A bunch

of jagged vertices. A seesaw in a hurricane. Either I'm so in love with myself that I crush people into dust, or I fall out of love with myself and off Mount Olympus into a crash-and-burn. I'm on this terrible, terrific roller coaster for life.

What you might find is that you've had at least one of these voices for a while, but you didn't have a name for it. Or you didn't know why you had it. Or you didn't know how much it was running the show. But I've learned that if you can name it and trace the source, you can take yourself back from the voices that are running you.

Each internal voice is a movement toward others or ourselves, either condemning or exalting. The diagram below is a four-quadrant model showing each movement and what they look like.

INTERNAL VOICES: VALUATIONS

	SELF	OTHERS
EXALTING	**SELF-EXALTATION:** Pride and Self-Justification	**EXALTING OTHERS:** People-Pleasing and Codependency
CONDEMNING	**SELF-CONDEMNATION:** Self-Doubt, Second-Guessing, and Insecurity	**CONDEMNING OTHERS:** Judgment, Resentment, and Controlling Others

Under "Self," we'll look at *self-exaltation,* the voice of pride. It has to get cracked first because it prevents us from looking inside altogether. Then we'll look at *self-condemnation,* the voice of self-doubt, which seems to be the loudest and most common. In the "Others" column, we'll discuss *exalting others,* the voice of people-pleasing, and *condemning others,* the voice of judgment, both of which are not what they appear to be. Finally, we'll look at how to balance these four voices.

Here's what I'm hoping: by the end of this part of the book, you'll be able to tell yourself, *I'm on to you.* You'll know why you fluctuate between extremes and what that means. You'll know why those voices are taking you for a ride, and why that's not always a terrible thing. You'll know how to turn them around for your benefit. We'll solve the mystery of what they're really saying.

No kidding, I'm excited to share this with you. What a journey it'll be.

CHAPTER 2

The Voice That Exalts You: A Cure No One Wants

Pride and Self-Justification

"Well, well," I said, "a tough guy."
— PHILIP MARLOWE, *THE BIG SLEEP*[1]

WHAT'S THE BIG IDEA?

One of the first things we learned in our chaplaincy program was that before we got to self-discovery, we had to deal with our defensiveness. Before we got to hear feedback about ourselves, we needed to deal with our inner attorney.

This was a lot harder than I thought it would be. I mean it. Offer somebody feedback and they can quickly pull a wise guy routine, the old "I don't know what you mean" alibi. Everyone seems to be real keen on humility, but mostly they want that for everyone *else*. Mostly people say *I'm a laidback guy*, but the second they hear criticism, they squirm. They stall with wildly fumbling explanations. They grip a shield that covers up and a sword that swings back.

You probably know someone who does this. You tried to bring up an issue, and they started throwing stuff.

In "The Trouble with X," C. S. Lewis talks about some irritating person X who makes your life miserable. You have tried to reason with him, but he covers his ears. Then Lewis delivers the plot twist:

> [There's] one more person of the same kind—the one you never do see. I mean, of course, yourself. That is the next great step in wisdom—to realize that you also are just that sort of person. You also have a fatal flaw in your character.[2]

There it is. You are X. I am X.

— — —

We each have a **voice of self-exaltation** in us that constantly threatens to armor up and attack. It looks a bit like bravado with a dash of insecurity. The engine that drives self-exaltation is *self-justification,* the need to explain our own actions so we can maintain a certain idea about ourselves.[3] Self-justification "minimizes our mistakes and bad decisions; it is also the reason that everyone can see a hypocrite in action except the hypocrite."[4]

The dilemma is that if you want to do surgery on the wounded ugly things inside, the defenses have to go down. For some of us, our guard is up so high that it covers our ears.

In our chaplaincy group, each of us had our turn at getting defensive. In particular, we had a guy who could dish it but he couldn't take it. He knew what was "best" for everyone but himself. That old story. A few months into the program, it all came to a head when I told him something a bit too much and he got in my face and started screaming.

At first I thought this sort of thing came from pride, and it sort of does—but I learned there was a deeper reason for these defenses. What I discovered underneath was sad and surprising. But also, hopeful.

"But Orrin says people ought to see themselves as they really are."
"Let's hope it never happens to him," I said.
— RAYMOND CHANDLER, *THE LITTLE SISTER*[5]

OH, I DON'T WANNA KNOW

I have to back up a little bit.

In our first month, we learned this idea called the Johari Window, created by two psychologists named Joe and Harry in the 1950s.[6] You might have heard about this, or if you are like me, you have used it against someone.

Our supervisor Audrey drew the Johari Window on a chalkboard: a box divided into four boxes, each with a different name.

Arena: the stuff you know about yourself and that's known to others.

Façade: the stuff you know about yourself but that's unknown to others.

Blind Spot: the stuff that others know about you but you don't know about yourself.

Unknown: the stuff that no one knows about, including you.

Then Audrey said, "I'm going to add a fifth box. It's the stuff you know about you but you don't *want* to know. It's the Known Unknown. That's the hardest box to deal with."

It was not just that we had blind spots, she said, but that we could be deliberately blind to those blind spots.

When our group time went into IPR, Interpersonal Relations, this was for the very purpose of seeing what we refused to see. We talked about each other's *growing edges.* Think of those suggestion boxes at restaurants, except there is no box and no fancy lighting and you get the feedback right in front of you. With eye contact and everything.

You get four or five other people telling you about yourself, telling you what could be better, and naturally you will get defensive and withdraw or shout your way out. I mean, who are you to tell me, anyway?

But when we dug in, we saw how rapidly we grew.

Trust the process, they kept saying.

That was our mantra. Our code. The Grand Law.

Audrey was the steady hand through the process. She was the reason I could trust it. She could say hard stuff but make it sound inviting, and she never judged anyone, not even for a second. If one of us said something that needed exploring, she would say, "I feel my stomach twisting. What do you think that means?" One time I suggested antacids. She said, "Humor, huh? What do you think *that* means?"

44

Always, Audrey repeated: *Trust the process.* Trust that we were here for a reason, to excavate what was going on inside.

Does that sound romantic to you?

It did to me—but none of us were as teachable as we thought we were. Our blind spots were miles wide and caverns deep.

Trust the process, they told us. Might as well have said, *You can catch the parachute on the way down. Good luck.*

— — —

In IPR, a typical conversation might have gone like this:

> CHAPLAIN ERICKA: I'm struggling with this, Brady. You say you can hear criticism just fine, except for when I just said you have a hard time with criticism. Is that something you can consider, at least?
>
> CHAPLAIN BRADY: Like I said, I'm fine with criticism. I like to hear it a certain way, though. You need to encourage me first, and then I'll hear it. In my opinion, you're all bad at criticizing. I saw you and J whispering and giggling in the hallway and rolling your eyes at me. Yesterday? Remember that?
>
> C. ERICKA: It was definitely something else. Brady, it sounds like you made up a story in your head.
>
> C. BRADY: It sounds like you're trying to make up a story in *my* head.
>
> SUPERVISOR: Hold on, Brady. What is your gut telling you about why they were laughing?
>
> C. BRADY: My gut says that you're all ganging up on me and you're a bunch of favoritists. You pick on me but you won't call her out?

45

The criticism bothered all of us, but there were some of us who went into a Shakespearean type monologue to defend themselves. You know, *doth protest too much* and the like. At that point, the discussion became a hazardous obstacle course. It was a stuck-at-an-impasse situation. The defensive person might say, "Sure, I'm open to hearing you," but once you held up a mirror, they would turn that mirror around and say, "Well, you know what *your* problem is—" and then back up with, "All I'm trying to say is—" and then finish with, "If you had only said it nicely, I would've heard you." Get through one hoop and up came another.

Look, I know I've done the same thing. All you have to do is point out a flaw in the design and my thumb starts looking for your eye socket. I've poked out plenty of eyes in my time. You've done that too, haven't you? Lunged at somebody who got too wise with you? Got your hackles up when someone challenged your beliefs and your winsome personality, which are all a work-in-progress and *None of your business, thank you and good day*?

I get it. We're creatures of self-preservation, after all. You have to protect your interests and guard the core part of yourself. You would be crazy not to. But the issue is that if you hermetically seal yourself off from every kind of suggestion, then you're not really accountable to your own errors. You end up speeding down the wrong way of a one-way at a hundred miles per hour wreaking havoc, all the while thinking you are much healthier than you really are.

YOU'LL HAVE TO GET THROUGH ME FIRST

Here are just a few defense mechanisms we use to insulate ourselves. You've probably used at least one of these.

Rationalization. *Justifying your behavior with illogical reasoning, i.e., excuse-making.*

> "I can quit any time. And cigarettes are just as bad as coffee."
>
> "She broke it off because I was too smart for her. I was going to break it off anyway. It wouldn't have worked anyway / she doesn't listen anyway / he was a jerk anyway."

Projecting. *Presuming about others what you actually have in yourself.*

> "Everything I do makes her hate me more."
>
> "She's cheating on me, I know it."
>
> "He's just jealous of me."

Blame-Shifting. *Offloading accountability on anyone and everything else. Also called "kicking the dog" or "passing the buck."*

> "You made me do it."
>
> "I was late because of traffic (they were late because they're rude)."
>
> "If it wasn't for my family / this city / my boss, then____."

Deflection. *Pinning the conflict on an irrelevant target (a strawman), usually to avoid self-awareness.*

> "Well-what-about-you?"

"This has nothing to do with me."

"You're the one who's _____."

Gas-lighting/Manipulating. *Constantly changing a standard with arbitrary goalposts to keep someone guessing.*

> "If you had just apologized / said it earlier / let me know, then I would've ____."
>
> "I didn't know you were so sensitive / touchy / humorless."
>
> "What I meant was ____."
>
> "I was just kidding around."

There's another one. If you read this list and at any point thought, *That's exactly what they do!*—then you may have weaponized the list to avoid looking at yourself.

— — —

Why is facing ourselves so hard? Don't we all want to hear the truth?

I would like to think so. But like Emily Dickinson said, "the truth must dazzle gradually, or every man be blind."[7]

This could mean that telling the truth needs a light touch, a soft tone, preferably lowercase letters. That helps. But for a person who isn't used to that sort of thing, it's hard to hear because they never had to. So when the truth comes around, it feels like the world is blowing up or something. That's not really their fault. No one had to sit them down and tell them that their opinions might be wrong sometimes.

This bias can develop into something called the *Dunning-*

Kruger Effect.[8] It's a bit of an overused term now, but the idea is that some of us have an inflated view of our own ability and a poor estimation of our weaknesses. In other words, we're generally not very skilled at observing our own lack of skill. You've probably seen this on shows like *American Idol* or *X-Factor* where some singer really has no idea what they sound like. For some of us, we might have "an unhealthy belief in our own importance," which leaves us refusing to improve.[9] But even when we admit there's room to improve, change is difficult: there's the Einstellung effect, which is the tendency for people to keep with their "tried and true methods" instead of changing for the better. The more we think we know, the less we will try some other way.[10]

But the main thing is, hearing feedback about yourself is hard. It's why we shrink-wrap ourselves with Dunning-Kruger and Einstellung and defense mechanisms. The very idea we're *wrong* feels awful. Most of us take it like a punch to the chest and walk around feeling bad for a while. You've probably seen them standing in the rain looking through a window or something. It might have been me. We can't help it.

A REAL FLIMSY FRAMEWORK

I used to think this was a narcissism problem. It's easy to jump to that word very quickly, and I do think there are a lot of self-absorbed people around that qualify. But I'm reminded of Brené Brown's take on "narcissists." She saw at least a few of them as people who had a hard time being vulnerable. She wrote,

> Our first inclination is to cure "the narcissists" by cutting them down to size ... [But] when I look at narcissism through the vulnerability lens, I see the shame-based fear of being ordinary. I see the fear of never feeling extraordinary enough to be noticed, to be lovable, to belong, or to cultivate a sense of purpose.[11]

In other words, I think there's a deeper reason we avoid looking at what needs to change. Self-exalters, I think, are reacting to the fear of inadequacy, the fear that they're not just wrong, but *intrinsically* wrong. In each of us is this unbearable spiritual dissonance that we're clawing to erase, a cosmic fracture that we smooth over with all sorts of justifications. It seems many of us have this intense fear of being perceived as weak or flawed because it was called shameful and ridiculous. So we use the ego to override our self-doubt. We trade one bad voice for another. It's a very popular thing to do.

That would mean the self-exalting person and the self-doubting person are the same coin in mid-flip. What we have was a grand cover-up. A masquerade of big shots barely keeping it together. What the Chinese Triads call "show face." *Everyone, I have learned, is a little bit terrified about our own worth and we use the tools we have to feel less scared.* Take anyone who is an over-confident showman or who talks in "teacher tones" or who gets mad when they hear that they're wrong, and most of the time they're just afraid. Afraid that they're small or incompetent or that people might see them. Like really see them.

Once you figure this out about people, they make a little more sense. Their huff-and-puff and eye-scratching are all survival tricks. They can't see through their blind spots because that would mean staring into an abyss of self-loathing. And I think you can have more empathy for defensive people once you know that they're dangling on a precipice all the time.

— — —

That was the thing. The defensiveness was a way to stay alive, maintaining all that person's self-worth, a series of clasps around a bursting heart. It's a flimsy framework waiting to collapse.

What I mean is, the ones who couldn't hear criticism didn't have the internal composition to stand such a thing. Psychologist Harriet Lerner says, "For people to look squarely at their harmful actions and to become genuinely accountable, they must have a platform of self-worth to stand on."[12] Organizational psychologist Tasha Eurich says that people who are highly aware of their own flaws—she calls them unicorns—must also be the most self-accepting.[13] Without self-acceptance, then, any sort of accountability is going to burn badly.

I think that's sad all around. Often a self-exalting person doesn't see anyone as equals—but they themselves have never felt equal to anyone, either. Because of that, they usually live on a perch alone.

DOWNTOWN SHOWDOWN

He had an opinion of himself, I think, that was too high for his own good. Or maybe it was the reverse. Maybe it was a low opinion that he kept trying to erase.

— TIM O'BRIEN, *THE THINGS THEY CARRIED*[14]

Here's how it happened.

Chaplain Brady was one of those guys who couldn't take it. We all told him the same thing because we saw the same thing. He couldn't see it—or didn't want to. At times I'd think he was living in some fantasy world where everyone had only catered to him.

"Brady, I think maybe you have a problem with Ericka."

"Brady, I think you're in denial. I think you're projecting. I think you're rationalizing."

"Brady, I think you offer great criticism, but you can't handle it so well."

He'd lash out, act out, and push back constantly.

But—*I get it*. I totally do.

I mean, can you imagine hearing all of that about yourself? Have you ever *had* anyone tell you about yourself?

So I get why Brady blew up. A few months into the program, he exploded. I had told him one more thing about his life that he didn't want to hear, and that was it.

Brady just came after me. Out of his chair and everything. He stood up and put his finger to my nose and got really red-faced and let the spit fly all over my necktie. And right then, my urge to shrink back really kicked in. Brady was my elder, after all. What did I know?

He was in my face, yelling, wagging his finger up and down my nose. "You said I was a bad chaplain, you said so!"

"No," I said. "I never said that."

"Yes, you did!"

"Brady," I said, with tears in my eyes. "I think that one's on you."

Brady put two of his fingertips on my forehead and shoved my head back as hard as he could. This guy, really. I had half a mind to slug him. He stormed out, not quietly.

I don't mean to make myself sound like the good guy here. I could've been the problem. Maybe I unfairly suggested that Brady was a bad chaplain. But if that was true of either of us, we could have talked about it instead of playing the old "Yes-you-are-No-I'm-not" game. I wish we had the chance. I wish we could've trusted each other.

A REAL HEARTBREAKER

I think *trust* was the issue. I would like to think that Brady just wasn't in the right place, and he could've trusted another group to say the things he needed to hear. Or maybe the program was too accelerated and condensed—and maybe one sit-down for Brady felt less like an intervention and more an inquisition. I had to wonder if our specific group reminded Brady of people he had dealt with before, who he had trusted once and they laid into him.

In fact, it's possible some of the defensive people you met *had* tried to be open to criticism before, but they got a Molotov truth-bomb. They had been burned by people who fancied themselves "truth-tellers," whether their mother or minister, and all that harsh nitpicking was still ringing in their ears. Even the kind words they heard were used to take advantage of them, so they couldn't hear the good stuff either.

The sad thing I learned is that the voice of exalting ourselves is often a safeguard put in place from a previous injury. We opened up in good faith and got a kick in the chest. So it comes down to this: *Unless we know we're safe, we'll never have the ears to hear truth or kindness or anything in between.*

In the bestselling *Crucial Conversations: Tools for Talking When Stakes Are High,* it's stated this way:

> People rarely become defensive simply because of *what you're saying. They only become defensive when they no longer feel safe. The problem is not the content of your message, but the condition of the conversation.*[15]

The honesty stings less when you can trust the other person enough to know that they're out for your good and not out to get you. There has to be a trust that says, *However which way we land, you're okay by me.* The only way to give and to handle criticism, it seems, is to first know that *no one will disconnect no matter what.* The weight of critique is too much to bear unless it's undergirded by people who stick around. Without unconditional connection—*counter-conditional,* really—there can be no trust. And without trust, no one can hear the hard things or even the good things.

Real accountability, then, happens when someone is willing to tell you how it really is but with tears in their eyes, voice shaking, heart breaking. Honesty can only happen in a culture of compassion, when you have the hope of reciprocal, unexpected welcoming, that our stories will be held with the care of a midwife and the skill of a surgeon, that we'll be embraced not by cringing but by grace.

The good news here is that safe, trustworthy people exist, and they know how to do this sort of honesty.

A WORD FOR YOU:

Give It to Me Straight

Here's what this looks like. There are two ways you're going to give or receive criticism, and you need both. One is a *shock* and one is a *stream*. Your response to those voices, and the way you offer them, will be crucial.

The *shock* is from somebody who drops off the criticism on your lap. You get a front-and-back anonymous note in your workplace or one of those unrestrained emails that let you have it. Your father-in-law or four-year-old makes a left-field comment about your hygiene. Or in a heated moment, you hear a remark that's really out to injure you. It's possible that 100 percent of these words are contrarian fluff. But there might be 2 percent of their words that *does* ring true. Just a kernel of them has a new and gracious path set out for you. Those truly are divine golden nuggets in a pile of stones. In cases of terrible wrapping, there's often a merciful gift.

Then there's the *stream*. That's when you allow yourself to be in a relational place, whether with a person or a group, that regularly exchanges criticism. In this case, a better term is *feedback*. That feedback is going to have *data* and *direction*. Data is real content, such as, "Last week at six in the evening, I ran into you at the corner of Main and Jefferson and you said a mean thing." Direction is actionable, which means *you can do something about it.* The feedback has to come from a *safe person*, someone who holds your past with compassion, your present with curiosity, and your future with a wide open vision.

That safe person, whether your spouse, a church elder, a childhood buddy, or a mentor, will hardly flinch at your worst. You'll know you're around a safe person because as they speak and listen, you'll feel the burden lift off your shoulders. You'll sigh in relief that you're not alone. Their honesty isn't just to sound tough, and it has enough light to point out your blind spots without making you blind. They can turn your tunnel vision into a panorama. I suppose they'll be much like Jesus, who somehow leads but also walks alongside, who speaks with authority but will wash your toenails with His sweater.

Sometimes the shock and stream come together. We had this policy among the chaplains that when somebody felt like they were slighted, they would try to resolve it right then and there. I wasn't used to that sort of confrontation. It was icky, a real sweat in the pits situation. But we aired things out right away, without the fear of getting socked in the nose. A few times a week, I would hear someone say, *That was weird, let's talk about that.* We were ready for the shock, always swimming in the stream.

At the moment you're confronted, you might get the palm twitch and stomach gurgles. There's always a burst of bodily reactions when the idea of yourself gets threatened. That's natural, I think. But there's still the matter of the feedback. You have the choice to take the person at his word, to see the hurt you caused, to recognize what you can do to turn it around. And if both of you are safe people, then something stunning will happen: *the confrontation will make both of you stronger because confrontation with a safe person can lead to growth.* A conflict with direction can always lead to transformation, both in you and in that relationship.

I've had friendships where the other person relished being harsh and over-righteous, who was always wiping blood from their fangs. They were not safe. Sometimes that guy was me, unfortunately, and people were right to leave. But I've had those other friendships where we endured the jagged road of seeing the worst in each other. It was ugly. Demons were exposed. Secrets were spilled. And still, we went the painful distance. We didn't pray, "God, make my friend open their eyes." We prayed, *"God, open my eyes so I can see my friend."*

You have to know that *self-awareness is only and fully found in the awareness of others.* It can't happen with only flattery and yes-men. You need brave people to step in and point out the things you've avoided. Without the people who are willing to confront you with the surgical truth, you will never be liberated from the lies you believe. Do you know a person like this? They *exist.* It's worth reconnecting with that friend who didn't see companionship as perpetual small talk and happy hour, but as an adventure of seeing the person they knew you could be. You can find that safe person. You can be one. It starts with humility. It runs on audacity. It takes more than once. It takes a lifetime.

Each of us can get to a place where we lay down our weapons. I know those weapons served you well. They helped you feel strong when you were weak. You didn't know you could be strong without them. You can.

Here's a summary of how to get through the defensiveness:

1. *Hear the hard things.* It will sting. A lot. Not all the hard things said are right, but most of them are worth hearing. There is at least one friend or one group that

can help you see what you can't. It will probably take more than one conversation.

2. *Check the defense.* Everybody has a way of protecting their own interests. That's a good thing, but it can also overprotect us, preventing us from uncomfortable truth. Explore the defensiveness and make space for the discomfort of words you've never considered before.

3. *Borrow someone's eyes.* Find a safe person or group. Meet regularly. Hear their honest wisdom. Don't wait: ask for feedback first. Ask as specifically as you can. Assume they can see more than you can. And trust them as much as you can stand it.

Trust the process, Audrey kept saying.

I trusted the process because I trusted my fellow chaplains. I believed we were on the same mission, the same page, with the same kind of urgency. I trusted we were here for the same reasons: to serve people, to serve each other, to grow and to go with God. There was no benefit in holding back. I probably wouldn't trust them if they did.

I learned a lot being open this way. It wasn't easy to hear the hard stuff, but it was harder not to.

The scary thing is that if you have to crack at your own defenses and take a look inside, you're liable to crash quickly. There's no limit to how much we can loathe ourselves. No kidding.

But we have to go there. That brings us to *the voice that condemns you.* If you're like me, it's as comfortable as a coffin and closer than the skin on your teeth.

CHAPTER 3

The Voice That Condemns You: I Wish I Had Just

Self-Doubt, Second-Guessing, and Insecurity

"So far I had only made four mistakes."
— PHILIP MARLOWE, *TROUBLE IS MY BUSINESS*[1]

ON THE LAM TO SPLITSVILLE

This is really embarrassing but in my second month of chaplaincy, I froze up in front of a whole family and panic-ran from the room. Ducked out, made my way to Splitsville. Like literally pushed people aside and ran down the hallway with my elbows pumping.

The program asked us to *pay attention to a disproportionate reaction* because it showed us an unresolved issue. I think running away from a room at full-speed was a pretty big hint about something.

The sprinting episode was a moment of revelatory truth, my *inciting incident*.

In a movie screenplay, the inciting incident is the first plot point that sets the story in motion. Like someone gets fired or falls in love or trapped in a building or finds out he's a wizard, and the rest of the movie is about the characters reacting. You find out what the characters are really made of, and in a good movie, you watch them change for the better.

Here's how my inciting incident happened. I was called to the ER where they brought in a kid who had broken his neck in a car accident. His family was in a private waiting room. When I got there, the family was spilling out of the room into the hallway, maybe fifty people in total. They were all crying and yelling and swaying and holding each other.

The family members in the hallway noticed me and they parted, letting me pass to the waiting room. They looked hopeful, expectant, like I had some magic words. I thought about all the things to say and not to say. And my stomach did a spin. A whole lot of voices rushed in, like a reverse clown car in my brain. It was familiar; I went through this routine all the time.

What if I say something stupid?

What if my voice comes off nasally and I do that loud nose-breathing thing?

What if I spontaneously trip into a table?

What if I sneeze?

What if I'm not the guy they need?

What if I don't have what it takes?

What if I'm not wearing pants right now?

Then the sweats. Hot fever. Stomach twisted. Hands jittery. Knees rubber. Mouth dry. All the usual symptoms. I also felt selfish. I knew this family was going through a lot more than my spiral of self-consciousness. I had to put myself on hold. Just shove down the panic attack and do my job. I made my way through the door. The room wasn't big but they managed a couple dozen people in there. Everyone was taller than me. Seriously, a land-of-Canaan-type situation. It was easy to tell who the parents were—they were on the couch, surrounded. The parents looked up and saw me, and they reached out their hands to hold mine.

"Chaplain, thank God you're here," the mother said. "Could you pray with us?"

The entire room turned to me. And right then my vision got funny and collapsed into a vignette, a shrinking pinpoint of sepia and purple and then nothing, and I could only hear the ridiculous thoughts in my head—*Can you do this? Are you good enough? What if you can't?*—and I took a step back. I thought I might go limp and fall over.

"I'm sorry," I said to no one. The words fell out in chunks. "There's another chaplain coming." I spun around and ran into someone and clawed at a bunch of people and generally made a fool of myself trying to jump out of the room and I scrambled into the hallway and leapt into a restroom and sat down on a toilet and leaned over for twenty minutes trying to catch my breath.

At times like these, my inner monologue is always the same—

What was that?

What is wrong with me?

Why am I like this?

YOU KNOW WHAT YOU'RE REALLY LIKE

The panic-run revealed a problem I always knew I had, **the voice of self-condemnation**. You know the one. It runs you down with self-doubt, self-loathing, second-guessing, insecurity, and a general sense that you're a no-good nobody.

I probably could've kept it all hidden, like professionals do—but the next day, I was called into the office. Another chaplain had reported me.

The family I had run away from requested a second chaplain, and he found out what had happened. In his report, he wrote, *Chaplain J. missed out on a powerful moment. I'm worried that his insecurity is limiting his capacity to offer his best.*

I was called into the office by Frida, one of the supervisors. Honestly, of all the supervisors, I was scared the most of Frida. She had this really piercing way about her, like if she looked at you too long, you might confess everything.

Before I could sit down, I blurted out, "I'm sorry. I choked. I totally choked."

I fell into a chair and put my head in my hands. I didn't cry or anything like that. I just wanted to jump in the wall and die.

Frida let me sit in the moment for a while. Then she said, "No shame here, I promise. I'm curious though . . . where do you think this came from?"

"It's that voice," I said. "The one that accuses you of being small and inadequate. It's the oldest story in the world. *I'm-not-enough* and that sort of thing. *You're not as good as you pretend to be. You know what you're really like. You'll mess this up.* It's ridiculous.

Existential panic. Melodrama in the brain. I just didn't know it was that bad. That room . . . it was too much."

"It was a tough place to be," she said, "and maybe it means that this job isn't for you. But I'm not sure that's true. I think you're a capable chaplain."

Frida paused. We sat there, letting the clock go, pressing into the moment.

"How do you see yourself right now?"

"I see this person I want to be—but then I look at who I *really* am, and it's a sad situation. I have this picture in my head of some super ideal version of me, but there's this *chasm* to get there. I think that's why I ran. I wanted to be some kind of amazing chaplain for this family, an A+ chaplain, you know? But there was no way I could deliver on that. So I had to run."

Frida smiled. A big smile. "Excuse me for saying this—*but you're just not that good*. Neither is anyone else. You were never going to deliver. At least not on this 'super ideal' version of you. If I had to live up to that, I would always doubt myself, too. Have you considered that your self-doubt is from putting an impossible demand on yourself?"

LIFE KEEPS SHOULD-ING ON ME

What Frida told me was true. I saw the same thing in dying people. On their deathbeds, they'd tell me about some version of a life they wish they had. Mostly I heard the same kinds of things on every deathbed: regret, lost time, the guilt. All the forks in the road. The things they did. Did not do. Were held back from. Almost had, but lost. Did well, until the end.

Mostly I heard:

I should have ____.

If only I had ____.

I wish I could have ____.

Many of us walk around this way. We're filled with the remorse of "should," with *imperative burdens.* You get the idea. At the end, your head is heavy with both the life you should have lived in spite of the one you did.

But I had to wonder: where did this idea of *should* come from?

HOSTILE ALLEYWAYS AND HEROIC DAYDREAMS

The more I try to get it right the more mixed up it gets.
—HARUKI MURAKAMI, *BLIND WILLOW, SLEEPING WOMAN*[2]

Frida recommended a book to me called *Neurosis and Human Growth* that laid out some of my fears. My wife got me the book for my birthday (you can imagine my friends' reactions) and I tore through it in a few days.[3]

The author of *Neurosis,* Karen Horney (pronounced *horn-eye*) says that early on, our self-worth can get robbed because of *adverse experiences* like trauma or abuse or exclusion or just plain falling short. So we fall into an anxiousness about everything. The world becomes a hostile and unpredictable battleground always threatening to steal more worth. The brain has to deal with this. It's supposed to fight for us—except it does this a little too well.[4]

To cope with the anxiety, our brains reach for an *idealized self,* a fantasy version of the person we want to be.[5] Almost like we say, "Never again, I'm going to be stronger and smarter and better than what happened to me." We attempt to re-create the sense of safety we may have had before the world got scary. The book lists certain *types* we try to become, like warrior, martyr, performer, or perfect mom. But taken too far, we enter into a kind of permanent daydream, envisioning ourselves in a grandiose salvation project. That's when *should* enters the crime scene. You look for what you *should* be, and you become a frustrated Venn diagram with two circles that stretch miles apart. Karen Horney says it like this: "The best way to describe the situation is in terms of **two people**. There is the unique, **ideal person**; and there is an omnipresent stranger (the **actual self**), always interfering, disturbing, embarrassing."[6]

When I read all this, I knew it was true. These ideas weren't brand new or anything, but they got to me because they accurately described *the madness of sprinting to be whole.* The itchiness of it. The pressure of it. Standing at the gap between *what you are* and *what you want to be,* and getting deflated every time you look across the chasm.

— — —

If you look around a bit, the *idealized self* is championed everywhere. Every motivational speech, book, and blog post is telling you how to put your best self into action. You hear another three-point sermon and piercing TED Talk and you read another list of "20 Things to Do Before You're 20," and that adds up to a billion ways to upgrade. It doesn't take a wild imagination to get caught up in the self-improvement game: everybody and their mother has a list of how you could be better.[7]

Besides that, with all the viral sensations online, it's easy to look at someone's peak highlights and get a distorted sense of success.[8] The idea going around is that everybody has to be a big hit or they're nothing. The social media stuff isn't wrong in itself, but it's one more way to compare yourself to a hyper ideal. You're always seeing someone's outlandish marriage proposal or vacation or carefully recorded act of charity. It's easy to get your worth mixed up with going viral, for the one hit of validating dopamine. Every new study on social media seems to have the same conclusion: *Look around and you'll shrink a whole foot.*

All of this fuels the same voice I heard on every deathbed. Over and over, hundreds of times, the constant comparison between *should* and *is.* None of it was surprising, but I was stunned by how *overbearing* that voice was in every patient I met, and in myself, and how much it made the walls close in. It was a universal agony, all this *should* stuff.

This explained why I was so hard on myself: I was holding myself hostage to the impossible. I was trying to be someone I was not—but even worse, someone I could *never* be.

THE DEADLIEST WALTZ:
PAS DE DEUX WITH IMAGINATION

I mean, it's good to dream and hope and all. It's one of the best things about us. Our imagination is endless. Our hearts run on possibilities. At the same time, that's the problem. Your brain can measure on a scale of infinity. It can see all the alternatives *ad nauseam*. The person you hope to become is a million different people.[9] My high-powered imagination was giving me a thousand different versions of things that never came to pass, and I was buckling under the gravity of all those dreams. Like W. B. Yeats said, *In dreams begin responsibilities*.[10] That's probably why the ending of the movie *La La Land* captures so many people. Everybody has imagined an alternate version of life, whether it was with a different partner, career, or city, or running away with Ingrid Bergman on a biplane.

You can waltz in with a plan and perfect intentions and some key performance indicators—those are all good things worth having, but they can become a kind of pressure chamber that doesn't allow room for mistakes. So you can end up freezing up before you enter a room or beating yourself up as you run out. Or you might perform out of fear, and the entire time you're a wreck and you replay it all shouting at yourself in the shower.

Here's an example of what I mean. The first time I ever called a girl, I was fourteen and I wrote an entire script of questions on a giant piece of cardboard. I thought that if I was silent, I had no personality. All the cool guys had something to say. I didn't breathe between questions. *What's your favorite color? How many siblings do you have? Star Wars or Star Trek? Boxers or briefs?* After a minute or two, it sounded like I was interrogating the poor girl. We never talked again.

This probably sounds a little funny, but if I could see my fourteen-year-old self in a movie scene, I would feel bad for the kid who was holding up the whole world with a piece of cardboard.

Self-condemnation at its very worst is a constant shame-spiral.

When you give in to that voice, you can fall into despair.[11] That persistent, gnawing sense of inadequacy. Checking out, giving up, flaking out. It's no wonder our brain had to dream up something better.

THE FALSE SOLUTION: MAKE-OVER MONTAGE

But what's so wrong with striving for the ideal, anyway? Why not dream? Hasn't that generally been the point of *life*?

At first glance, we might say that "striving for your best self" is not a bad idea. I would agree. It's a pretty fine idea and it can work for a while. A high chin can open some doors. Striving for excellence is an important part of the human story.

The problem is that there's a way of getting better that isn't getting better, but is only "ruthlessly marching over an anxiety,"[12] like whistling past a graveyard. Like dressing up a ghost. It doesn't address the original issue—the fracture inside that caused the anxiety in the first place—and in the long run, it's a set-up for a crash.[13] You can jump between mountain peaks as long as your knees will take it, but at some point, that will lead to a steep drop off two different cliffs.

THERE'S BEEN A BREAK-IN: A HOLOGRAM CAPER

The first cliff—the first problem—with the idealized self is that reality breaks in.

As long as we stay ahead, we have the trophies to prove ourselves—but eventually, we hit our limits. Inevitably, irrevocably, we fail and get rejected. Things don't work out. Other people get ahead of us. Time and aging do their thing. The checklist goes unchecked. We get shipwrecked. Or as Karen Horney says, "Usually the reality of himself intrudes painfully and unmistakably ... [Then the] actual self becomes the victim of the proud idealized self."[14]

In the final boxing match of the movie *Creed*, Rocky, the famous boxer turned trainer, is about to throw in the towel for his apprentice, Adonis "Donnie" Creed. Donnie, the illegitimate son of champion Apollo Creed, tells Rocky not to stop the match. He finally reveals his entire motivation.[15]

> DONNIE: Don't, okay? Let me finish. I got to prove it.
>
> ROCKY: Prove what?
>
> DONNIE: That I'm not a mistake.

I get it. I was a mistake too. And I guess that sort of motive can work for a round or two. But how about the long run? What if he had gotten knocked out in the first round? What does he do when he retires at thirty-five or pulls a hamstring really hard?

When life unfolds, your dreams can bust open. The hologram of the *idealized self* can fade and you'll be left with the *empirical self*, the evidence piled against you. The truth is laid bare: *I have a rap sheet the length of my torso. I have failed at so many things that no attorney would touch my case.* Over a lifetime, you accumulate a catalogue of setbacks, blow-ups, and disappointments. At each failure, the little voice chimes in, *See? That's really you. You never had what it takes.*

YOU OUGHT TO SEE A MIRROR SOME TIME

The second problem with the idealized self is that the more you achieve, the more you tend to feel like a fraud.

I heard this was a phenomenon called the Imposter Syndrome, that the people at "the top"—and lots of the rest of us—feel like it's all a fluke and they're due for a shakedown. It's easy to chalk up our wins to luck or timing or charm. So there's a double-bind: when I mess up, I beat myself up, but when I do a good job, I beat myself up even more. The little voice keeps accusing me, *Around the corner they'll find out you barely know what you're doing.*

I thought I was alone in this, but about seven out of ten people feel like they're faking their way through the world, like their accomplishments are tainted.[16] And the more the success, the greater the pressure to measure up to the applause. All the trophies and medals and awards get spun on a stick, announcing a version of you that's mostly spin.

— — —

I talked with Eugene Cho, founder of One Day's Wages and Quest Church in Seattle, who had something to say about this. He has raised hundreds of thousands of dollars to provide clean water and disaster relief and to fight human trafficking, and his social media altogether probably has a million followers. But I was surprised that he didn't think he was all that successful. I thought maybe it was a modesty thing, but he was serious. He told me:

> I just imagined that when I got to a certain place, certain accomplishments, certain whatever-it-could-be, that I'd feel super confident and super secure. And lo and behold, I still struggle with insecurity and doubt—maybe even more now than ever before. Which is surprising. I don't feel good about that.[17]

What I expected to hear was that when he was in self-doubt, he could just sort of inventory his own success and he would no longer feel like an imposter. But instead what he said was sort of the opposite: he took inventory of his stripped down self.

> Most people here at the church, they love me and they respect me, but I'm like Joe Schmoe to them. Occasionally a couple of my staff or my kids have traveled with me to conferences, and they're shocked. They'll come away going, "So what's going on here? Why are people lined up to meet you and take photos with you?" I need this. I need to have a group of people where I can be true to who I am. When I go speak somewhere, I'm going to put on a nice jacket, a nice pair of pants. But are there people that I can be with in Monday morning hair and sweats and it's totally okay? In other words, I think we still have to be in honest community.[18]

I suppose it sounds a little mean-spirited that Pastor Eugene's staff and kids were raising their eyebrows and all. I'm sure it was awfully humbling. But I also thought it was a relief for him, that he had a home base where nobody expected him in a pressed suit for a photo op all the time. He didn't have the pressure, with at least a select few, of being a hotshot speaker. His staff and kids apparently liked him with his human hair. One study suggests the same idea: students who got social support from people who knew them *outside* their field, like family and friends, felt more supported than by peers inside their field.[19] Those students had to flex around other students, but could relax around people who had long ago accepted them. So if the Impostor Syndrome says, *Around the corner they'll find out who you are,* and around the corner you have some people who already know who you are, then you sort of beat the syndrome to the punch. You wouldn't have to hold yourself up like a backwards Atlas so much.

That sort of honesty was key in not only dealing with the impostor business, but the idealized self too.

MODUS OPERANDI FOR FAILURE:
HOLDING THE HOT POTATO

In my chaplain group, we learned to shed our success-suits and let the reality of ourselves fully break in.

At the end of the supervision about my runaway visit, Frida asked me another question: "What do you think it would've been like if you stayed in the visit but 'messed up' anyway?"

"I guess they never would've called for a chaplain again," I said.

"And then?"

"Then I would've felt terrible."

"Then?"

"Then I would've died, I guess." I laughed.

Frida did, too. But her brow furrowed, a real look of concern. "That's the risk, isn't it? You might fail. They might leave. No one may understand you. It might all go wrong. It really is scary. Sometimes you just fail. And it hurts. It hurts. And it hurts."

Frida was doing a sort of exposure therapy. We did the same sort of thing in our group time. We spoke our failures out loud. We held the hot potato of our absolute blunders as long as we could. Long enough to burn.

It was not a pleasant thing. We would play out the worst case scenario. We grieved over our humiliating episodes and the ones in queue. And we made our imaginations work for us instead of against us, not by conjuring bigger ideals, but by working through the full heat of our failures, as crazy as that was. Nobody became a failure whisperer. Nobody would move in with a pep talk or solutions. Nobody said, "The worst case isn't so bad, see?" Because the worst case is *always* bad. But by getting burned by failure, we learned that this is how it goes sometimes. Reality breaks in, regardless of all the things we try to stop it with. *And so we learned to hold up failure as an event, separate from ourselves, as a thing we go through and not a thing that we are.* Of course, we might have made some poor choices. But we're limited, flawed, funny little beings. We fail. It's unavoidable. And it hurts.

Maybe this sounds like reveling in a big crying fest or something. Sometimes it was. But we were finally able to relieve the burden of expectations—mainly, our own.

Have you had a chance to do this sort of thing? How long have you been throwing hot potatoes across the room?

> *It is possible to commit no mistakes and still lose.*
> *That is not a weakness; that is life.*
> —JEAN-LUC PICARD, "PEAK PERFORMANCE"[20]

This experiment was done in Germany to help anxious test-takers with their test anxiety. The usual experiment would try to increase confidence by affirming with positive words, which is called *competence priming*. Like you might expect, it works. But in this new experiment, the participants were instead primed with "failure activation." They were given negative words to memorize before a test, words like *flop, failure, disappointment, break down, collapse,* and *debacle.*

The test-takers who were given "failure activation" did better and reported reduced anxiety. By becoming okay with failure, they ended up succeeding all the more. But there was something else: a twist was added. A group of test-takers were told to actively forget the negative words, *and the ones who tried to actively forget the negative words did worse on the tests.* Suppressing the notion of failure ironically made it more likely to fail. The ones who rolled around failure in their mouths became more comfortable with the idea.[21] The idea that every good effort can end in dust. It's a downer, I know. It's a painful, brutal truth. But like any truth, it will free you from a lie: that somehow it was all up to you.

THE LONG GOODBYE: FAREWELL, MY LOVELY

Here's where I landed.

The bad news was that I couldn't do all the things I had hoped to. *The good news was that I couldn't do all the things I had hoped to.* That was terrifying, but also liberating. I knew I could never get to saying, *I am enough.* The truth was, *I am **not** enough a lot of the time, and that's just fine.*

That would start with burying the ideal. All those demands and expectations and absurd parameters needed to be laid down. I needed to mourn my "best self." To grieve him. To say goodbye. I mean, that guy is great. Really. He knows what to say at parties and he cracks the right one-liners and he knows the difference between appetizers and hors d'oeuvres. He doesn't choke. He carries a room. He gets things done. I looked up to him. But up close, he was made of sand and old driftwood. A bloated mannequin. He was a concoction of every *should* and *have-to* and *you'd-better-or-else* whirling around in my head. More importantly, he simply was not me. I was never the kind of guy he wanted me to be.

If I could attend his funeral, I would have a much more accurate view of myself, and in turn no longer hide my flaws under a fantasy. In other words, if I could lay down my idealized self and embrace my limitations, I could learn to like the person I really was and figure out where I needed help. Maybe then I could fail without it crushing me. Maybe then I'd feel like less of an impostor, because I wasn't trying to be everybody's idea of what I *should* be. Maybe then I could quit running myself ragged up the side of a cliff called perfection. I could even enjoy my own success once in a while.

I know that all this time, my brain was just trying to protect me. It had to try. It had to give me an older brother to aspire to, who tried to make up for all the old hurt and anxiety and trauma. My brain had given birth to a champion who would fight for me in the schoolyard—but without meaning to, he overshadowed everything I did. He demanded blood. He gave birth to these condemning voices in my head. I really can't blame him. How would he have known? He was a great guy. A little too great. He was terribly perfect. And when I was okay with *good*, I didn't need him anymore. He left on his own. He eventually saw it in my face: that I would be okay without him.

> *"And now that you don't have to be perfect, you can be good.*
> *Is that it?"*
> *"I guess so. Maybe that's it."*
> — JOHN STEINBECK, *EAST OF EDEN*[22]

HE WAS ALMOST GREAT: HE WAS GOOD

I'm reminded of Paul from the Bible, who had something so grotesquely wrong with him that he had to bring it up all the time. If he didn't, his disciples would. The people of that day looked at a guy like Paul and could only think, *How can this guy run the show?* So Paul had a kind of self-awareness about how other people saw him. He wrote that he had a "thorn" in his side. It was probably a bunch of things: he mentions his bad eyes, and he's called a weak preacher, and he gets concussed once or twice by stoning, and he always seems to have some kind of flu.[23] Whatever his *thorn* might have been, it was obvious to people the second he walked in. He was a bug-eyed, bone-headed, mush-mouthed preacher.

There is that verse where Paul asks God to take away the thorn three times, and I don't know if Paul said, "Okay, it's been three days in a row now," or if it was more like three entire seasons of Paul just praying on his face begging for mercy. It must have been a hard thing when Paul was healing other people of illness and disability and demons, but he couldn't do anything about himself. He ends up making peace with God about that. Like he knows he'll have to move through the world in a broken state and it won't be pretty and he'll probably have to explain himself a lot. But still, he shows up. He says, *"For when I am weak, then I am strong."*[24] That's a crazy thing to say, I think, for most people. But he quits praying about some perfect life and settles into his own skin. And God works within those limits, or even through them. It was astounding, and still is, that God worked through nobody's idealized version of a strong person. So real strength, it seems, is never something that we would dream. In God's sort of dreaming, He flexes through weakness, through the least likely, even through someone like you and like me.

— — —

I met a patient named Danny who weighed 1,400 lbs. and was confined to his bed. His legs were amputated below the knees and he was going blind. He had a neurological deficiency in which he couldn't stop eating; he had become diabetic and was recovering from Takotsubo cardiomyopathy or, as it's also called, broken heart syndrome.

"Chaplain, I just think," he said, voice booming, "I was meant to do something. *Anything*. Not this. Everyone tells you that your life is meant for something great, but how can I do that here? Look at me."

"I'm sorry," I told him. Then I asked him, "What would it look like to do something from where you are?"

"From where I am?"

77

"I mean, instead of where you want to be . . . just from where you are."

"Hah," he said. "Hah," he said again.

The next evening, Danny asked for me to come by.

"I got it, chaplain," was the first thing he said. "I ordered ten pizzas." He quickly said, "Not for *me*, chaplain. Come on. For the whole floor. I figured that's the best I can do."

I nodded. "I think it's even better than that."

"Hah," Danny said, reaching for my hand. "I know I'll never get out of here, chaplain. But I'm here. One thing I'm trusting is that God sees me. He sees what I'm trying to do. I'm content with that. I'm very content with that. By the way, you want a slice?"

"Danny, I would love a slice. I would love a couple of slices."

— — —

I've met a lot of patients like Danny. Disease, disaster, disability: all of it robbed them. Those patients had the haunted look of missing the only turn on a one-way, a permanent phantom pain hovering at the edge of their skin.

But wasn't there hope for them? Did they have no value apart from their dreams?

What Danny taught me is that *real confidence comes out of contentment.* You might spend a lot of energy trying to be somebody great, to break through the doors of success, when a few doors down can be just as good. There's dignity in the hallway. You might find it hard to do even that much if you've been forced into the unforgiving edges of a measuring cup. But the ones I met who were *content* didn't speak about their lives in a metric quantity; it was more of a permeation of being. Like describing an aroma. A kind of humming song. And like many good songs, a lot is improvised. You can belt those blues any way you like just fine.

The world, as it is, can be so cruel and unfair. But we do what we can with who we are. We can share pizza with the whole floor.

> *But by the grace of God I am what I am:*
> *and his grace*
> *which was bestowed upon me*
> *was not in vain;*
> *but I laboured more abundantly than they all:*
> *yet not I, but the grace of God which was with me.*
> —PAUL OF TARSUS,
> THE FIRST LETTER TO THE CORINTHIAN CHURCH[25]

A WORD FOR YOU:

Tell Somebody What You Look Like

If you feel like an imposter right now, I think the best thing to do is to let everybody know. Give no quarter to impostorism. Show everybody what you look like. Maybe it's all been an act and you feel like a schlub down deep. That's perfect, because it isn't. I don't want the hero story. I want the schlub story. That's the good stuff.

Even when you find success and all, it's good to be around people who don't think you're such a big deal. Somebody who can see you with the Monday morning hair and falling on your face and crying about it. You still need people close to you who know you have a ways to go.

The thing is, when you start expressing the sheer embarrassment of your shortcomings out loud, you find you're not alone. That sounds corny, sure, but it's no less true. You find a lot of people who are also pretending, holding up a pretense of having it all together. By speaking your failures out loud, you dull its fangs. You loosen its grip. You rob it of its mythical power. And that confession is contagious. The people around you start to feel safe enough to drop their perfectionist armor.

I don't mean you roll around in self-pity or anything. I mean that once in a while you can let somebody see behind the idealized curtain. A real Wizard of Oz type moment. Except you choose to reveal yourself. What a relief that would be to quit pulling all those levers. You'd be free of that garish projection of yourself on a soundstage. You'd be an ordinary vulnerable person just as scared as everyone else. And that would be extraordinary, really. I wish I had people like that around me back then, who were afraid to tell their real story but they did anyway, in all its raggedy detail, and by weakness became strong.

Here it is: There's a kind of false strength that forces a distance between people because it's flexing so hard. It ends in a strange stalemate where everybody's muscles are popping out their sides, and nobody has room enough to breathe. But there's a kind of true strength that draws people closer. It's the strength of getting vulnerable, truthful, real. To be open enough to say, *Here's what I really look like.* When you admit weakness, you find a restful strength. A sort of unclenched relaxation.

You're probably craving that sort of thing. You don't have to wait for it. You could step out from the curtain any time now. In that weakness we find strength, and each other.

> *But he said to me,*
> *"My grace is sufficient for you,*
> *for my power is made perfect in weakness."*
> —PAUL OF TARSUS,
> THE SECOND LETTER TO THE CORINTHIAN CHURCH[26]

Here are three things that will set you free.

Bury the ideal. You can say goodbye, a little at a time, to impossible demands and romanticized plans. It's okay to feel hurt about that.

Face failure head-on. Things won't go the way you expect. There are no ideal outcomes. You can do good for a while, but the good can fall apart, too. It's okay to feel bad about that.

Celebrate in the hallway. Your idea of success will be different than you had dreamed, but that different version is worth enjoying. It's okay to feel good about that.

RETURN FROM SPLITSVILLE

A few months after I panic-ran from the waiting room, the chaplains were tasked with an experimental assignment:

The next time a patient dies in a Code Blue, pause the medical team and call for a moment of silence.

It was a terrifying proposition. I knew I had to do it.

Maybe this doesn't sound so bad, but you have to imagine a room full of doctors, nurses, and surgeons, finally facing a flat line, circling around somebody they've been trying to raise back to life for the last two hours—and in a whirlwind of wheels, beeps, syringes, tubes, gauze, and gloves, the clergy tells everyone to stop. I was all kinds of nervous. I kept thinking of their eyes and masks turning to me, burning holes in my frame. I kept thinking I would choke again, would grow another nose, run off to Splitsville again, go on the lam for good.

I got paged. It was time.

When I got there, I recognized the patient. It was one of the people I had run from in the waiting room. I mean, of course it was. And for a razor sharp moment, I knew this whole crazy enterprise was bigger than my own fears. It was about this patient. This person. I was called here. Maybe I'd mess it up, maybe I'd somersault on my face, maybe my voice would shake. But I wouldn't run again.

What little voice I had to give, I could give because it was for my patient.

A doctor called it. Time of death, about three in the morning. They had tried for over two hours, compressions and chemicals and everything.

"Hey," I said. "Hey."

They turned slowly, this tired team.

"I'd like to . . ."

My heart was pounding. And I saw one of the nurses, Freddie, give me a nod. Allie and Brenda, too. They needed it.

". . . I'd like to call for a moment of silence to honor the work done here, and to honor the life of Linda."

We closed our eyes. Thirty long seconds. I heard someone sniffle. Maybe allergies, or maybe they meant it. I was sweating, feverish. But mostly I was thinking of how proud I was of this team and that not everything turns out the way we want—but still, we throw into the ring, every ounce, we show up in there.

"Thank you, everyone. Appreciate each of you."

My voice cracked. It didn't seem to matter. They came up to me. Freddie, Allie, Brenda. A physician. A surgeon. They shook my hand. Freddie's eyes brimmed red. He told me, "That meant a lot, to know her name. Linda. Thanks for showing up, chap."

CHAPTER 4

The Voice
That Exalts Others:
All My Heroes
Are Everyone

People-Pleasing and Codependency

> *"Tall, aren't you?" she said.*
> *"I didn't mean to be."*
>
> — RAYMOND CHANDLER, *THE BIG SLEEP*[1]

A REAL KICK IN THE HEAD

Of all the voices, this one might have caused me the most trouble with my coworkers. The scary thing is that this voice, at its worst, was feeding an addiction. It was my coworkers who got me clean and sober.

It started with my fellow chaplain Ericka who told me:

"You're a people-pleaser."

She had finally gotten sick of my thin ice ballet. She got tired of my polite smiling and the constant *yes* to everything.

"You're a people-pleaser," she said again.

"Am I?"

"You are."

"I am."

"Are you saying that just to agree with me?"

"Am I?"

"Are you?"

I was. It was true.

I was brushing up against a lifelong problem, a real kick in the head. I'm a codepender. An approval-seeker. A pushover. A people-pleaser. I try to do what everyone else wants. I struggle with the **voice of exalting others**.

Here's why Ericka was telling me this. A few days earlier, she had asked me for help because she got swamped in the ER, so I told her, "I'm on my way." I ended up saying *yes* to five other things first. I arrived late. It got worse from there. Ericka needed help with a visitor who was being unruly. But instead of sticking up for Ericka, I got all friendly with the visitor: *Nothing is wrong, we're all cool, I'm your best friend*. It had the adverse effect of making Ericka look like some kind of villain while I was over here swooping in with my nice guy routine.

Because of my code-switching con job, I became a two-faced double-crosser. By trying to please people all the time, I was pleasing nobody. I soon got the reputation of being a fake and a flake. All this culminated in the IPR when Ericka told me, *You're a people-pleaser.* She landed one final punch: "If this is your way of earning validation, I just can't trust you. *You need to speak what's true, anyway.*"

I knew what she meant. If I was bending my will to the highest bidder, who can trust a guy like that? And what would be left of me?

— — —

Most people would say I was nice or easygoing or laidback—but that was because I could not stand to upset anyone. Like Brené Brown said, "I agreed to do something for someone for the wrong reasons. I wasn't being generous or kind. I said yes to be likable and to avoid being seen as 'difficult.'"[2] I was like Jackie Chan in every one of his movies: *I don't want any trouble.*

The sad part of it was, I was happy to keep my head low and open all the doors. I would stay quiet thinking I was doing everybody a favor. I liked the rush of pleasing others. I don't think it's entirely wrong to feel good about that. The only thing it cost me was myself. That was a small price to pay. Or so I thought, anyway. I would have been fine paying it—but it turns out, staying quiet also had a big cost to the very people I was serving.

> *You can't please all the people all the time.*
> *And last night, all those people were at my show.*
> —MITCH HEDBERG[3]

TELL ME WHAT YOU WANT: I'LL BE THAT

I can't exaggerate how much this people-pleasing thing is a problem for me. It's bad enough to make you blush. Audrey first noticed it when she shadowed me on a shift and observed that I *always* made a reference to a popular movie or TV show or actor or musician. She asked me why, and I blurted out, *So the patient won't think I'm too foreign.*

I get into this feedback loop about what everyone is thinking about me all the time. My entire being is enmeshed in the breath of others. People, it seems, are my drug. I like it when people like me. It's a real addiction. I look up at everybody with these floppy fish eyes and I get high off the slightest glance. If I find out some-one said an ill word about me, I die inside. My heart just withers. If you're like me, you know what I mean. You fall hard. Not in love, no, but in line. Waiting, hoping to get that glance.

My people-pleasing thing could be summed up from the book *Boundaries*:

> This type of boundary conflict is called *compliance.* Compliant people have fuzzy and indistinct boundaries; they "melt" into the demands and needs of other people.
>
> Compliants, for example, pretend to like the same restaurants and movies their friends do "just to get along." They minimize their differences with others so as not to rock the boat. Compliants are chameleons. After a while it's hard to distinguish them from their environment.[4]

This idea of compliance, of *melting into other people,* is shown by the Asch conformity experiments. A participant is shown several lines and has to match the two lines of equal size. But there are other people in the room who are in on the experiment, and they deliberately match the wrong lines. You can guess what happens: three out of four participants pick the wrong lines because everyone else does.[5]

Another experiment I read about showed that people with *sociotropy*, or those who are overly invested in others (the opposite of sociopathy), have a tendency to eat the same amount of food as everybody at the table,[6] or will even eat high-calorie foods if their friend does to help them feel less guilty.[7] I suppose that's me. A sociotrope. A chameleon. A beige reptile sticking to the walls.

Here's what it came down to: I had no power over my *yes* and *no*. I tended to say *yes* to all the wrong stuff and *no* to all the right stuff, all in hopes of looking like I was a team player. Yes, I like mayo. Yes, that racist joke is funny. Yes, I can work the extra few hours. Yes, I am fine. Yes, you are completely right. Yes, I ordered extra mayo. Yes, I can handle those twelve contradictory things you asked me to do by tonight.

I was afraid if I said *no*, I would get the mean stare. The stiff, sour look of rejection. That was worse than anything, to see people leave. I equated saying *no* to people as saying *no* to my own worth somehow. So I could not do what I ought to or even what I wanted to. It was a backwards situation.

SHE USED TO BE SO NICE

I am afraid to tell you who I am,
because, if I tell you who I am,
you may not like who I am,
and it's all that I have.

— JOHN POWELL, *WHY AM I AFRAID TO TELL YOU WHO I AM?*[8]

If you've gotten this far, you might think this people-pleasing stuff has an easy fix. You might tell me the solution is to stick up my chin, straighten my sternum, look these guys in the eye. Speak up for yourself, why don't you? Stop giving so much, will you? And I wish I could tell you I can get brave when I have to. "Oh brother," you might say, "I would give them a piece of my mind, you can believe that." And I believe that. But I've seen that the toughest of tough guys have at least one person—a boss, their mother, their sibling or child or hometown friend—who they crumble around easily. They turn jellyfish.

In fact, I'd say just about everybody cares how they're perceived: when two groups of people, one that claimed they cared a lot about others' opinions and one that didn't at all were given (faked) low scores for a presentation, they both reported nearly the same levels of lowered self-esteem.[9] I get that. Every tough guy gets weak at the knees with *somebody*. A spine has to bend somewhere. I'm the kind of guy who gets weak everywhere.

Here's the other thing. Many of us *have* tried to speak up before and got burned. Trying to "be yourself" sounds real nice, but it doesn't go over well most of the time. You dared to speak up and you got fired. You told your spouse or kids or parents or boss about your needs and they went to war. Or they made light of it. The regular: *Don't be that guy. Don't complain. You're overreacting. Count to ten. Take a nap.* You called for the manager and you were called spoiled. You got a little loud and somebody said, "Get a hold of yourself, you're making a scene."

So you backed off. Or maybe you yelled back and it got carried away and you lost the original thing you were trying to say. None of it seemed worth the trouble.

I've learned this the hard way. Most organizations I've known have pummeled people to play ball and keep bumbling along. Those places reward conformity. Most institutions want you to stay mum and over-commit. By default, there is a constant, inexorable pull into stillness. Either you must comply with standards or you'll be seen as "difficult" and "a maverick."

This is true with the business world, churches, celebrity circles, the HOA, and your own dinner table. This is especially and unfortunately true if you're a woman or a minority: research shows your confidence will mostly be seen as arrogance, and if you have a bad day, you're seen as "hysterical" or a "threat."[10] Some have to put on disarming mechanisms like a literal baby-face to appear friendly.[11] A child figures out quickly when to hush their own distress to keep everyone free of stress.[12] It's a survival mechanism. Some people can't wait to "tell someone off," but I can. I can hold a smile for a long time.

I'm not saying that we need to say every single thing that's on our minds all the time. But I think most of us have been so conditioned for *silence* that expressing even our most basic needs is an uphill task of comedic and tragic proportions. In environments where everyone is expendable and has to over-extend, the people-pleasers get thrown in a vise. The entire set-up is rigged. If you happen to be the guy who speaks up, you will get the seat closest to the door. So in one sense, a people-pleaser might have chosen to be that way. But in another sense, how could they have chosen to be anything else?

It's not enough, I learned, for one person to stand up and say, *I'm my own person now, see? I got a lot to say, who wants to know?* The immediate environment has to be open to that sort of thing.

DOWN THESE MEAN STREETS:
WE CAN MAKE IT, YOU AND I

In our chaplain group time, here was our operating agreement: *We encouraged each other to advocate for ourselves.*

We'd name a situation where we were silent about our injury and then give ourselves a redo. Most of the time, that meant we had to get mad. To own the anger that we already had.

Then we were asked a question:

What was the thing you really wanted to say?

We were given permission to vent the angriest, craziest, most outrageous stuff bouncing around in our heads. All the things you say in your imaginary midnight arguments—we were given a moment to say those things out loud.[13] Can you imagine? Have you done a thing like that? I'm telling you, it's like opening a window to the ocean.

I know that anger can be harmful and abusive. Many of us do get mad the wrong way. But I believe there's a healthy kind of anger which comes from a real place, from the place where our wounds were buried.[14] And really, the anger was pointing to a truth: *That was wrong and I didn't like it.* And deeper than that, *I have needs and you need to hear me.*

By having a space where we could speak those things out loud, we were practicing a skill called *congruency,* the degree to which our internal needs are expressed. It turns out, I had low congruency. I might as well have been a guy with no needs. I had never been asked, *What was the thing you really wanted to say?* Most of us, even given the permission, stammered through our venting and got sweaty in the face and laughed nervously with our hands doing things beyond our elbows. You've never seen a guy picking at his own collar so much until you've seen me trying to get out the words:

I need your help right now.

I need you to know that you hurt me.

I need you to stop lecturing me right now.

I need space right now.

I need you to try differently with me.

In chaplaincy, I could finally speak up. They would let me get mad. I mean that, with crazy gratitude. There was no fear of retaliation, no dread of losing my spot. They didn't let me squeak by on thin ice. They were my recovery group pulling me out of approval-addiction.

We need that sort of place, where nobody deifies anybody in fear of punishment, but also where everybody has relinquished any god-like status. There, nobody is chasing approval or withholding it, and we can say what we need.

— — —

Here's how it happens. Earlier I mentioned the Asch conformity experiment, the one where the participants would conform to everyone else's wrong responses. The experimenter wanted to find a way to break the conformity. So a small twist was thrown in: have just *one other person* in the room pick the right response. The results changed drastically. Instead of three out of four conforming, only five out of one hundred participants conformed. Having one person break out of the crowd was enough to topple the crowd. That one person was called a True Partner.

My workplace was full of True Partners. They knew that I was addicted to approval. They knew I physically had a hard time saying *no*. So they constantly clarified my *yes*. They would ask: *What do you need right now? What exactly do you want? How are you feeling about this? Really, what do you need? No, really, what do you need?*

In the hospital we were always figuring out: *is this in line with your abilities and limits and choices?* We were encouraged to draw clear boundaries around all the ways we could and could not operate.

And always, *What is the thing you really want to say?*

I don't mean that other people are responsible for your stuff. And the chaplains were not happy about this arrangement all the time; it takes a lot of emotional capital to talk so freely and to hear *no*. But for me, I cannot imagine going back to how it used to be—to how *I* used to be. Among the chaplains, I was for once in a healthy environment. The freedom was palpable. I was surrounded by people who risked comfort all the time to have authenticity. I was with people who cultivated a direct and transparent space to get ugly. That, to me, is the craziest kind of paradise I could imagine—and I wish it was the norm all over. It sounds impossible, but I'm telling you, I found Eden.

YOU OWE YOURSELF A FAVOR: NO MORE FAVORS

The reality, of course, is that "saying the thing you want to say" will get you rejected as fast as you can open your mouth. So at the heart of people-pleasing is a dilemma. You have two opposing needs. If you're like me, you need to keep people happy—but you also have a need for your own well-being. Unfortunately, very often one of these things will cost the other.

I'll put it another way. *A people-pleaser needs a controllable world of people who are satisfied, and they're willing to sacrifice themselves to have that controllable world.*

This "need" was born because the world can seem so out of control. So to keep people happy means you get a predictable row of faces always doting, praising, affirming. It seems like a good deal: sacrifice yourself to gain safety and smiling. But you probably see the irony. *It's impossible to stay safe when you have to maintain somebody's emotional weight.* Like I once heard, *Only God can be pleased. Everyone else has to be kept that way.* To keep them that way is not safety, but a stand-off. And if your connection with a person is contingent on your saying *yes* all the time, that's not a connection. That's coercion. It's conditional, on both ends. It's not sustainable.

The thing is that it's not wrong to serve people and to see them happy. But it gets selfish when the agenda is, *They have to like me so I can feel okay about myself.* I used my service as a way to control others, so I could feel in control. I had to give up the big idea that I would be safe if I could hold off everybody's rejection.

I was at least partially responsible for setting up that dynamic. Which meant I could make the choice to change it too.

In my earlier example, I mentioned that I said *yes* to a bunch of different chaplains at once, stretching myself too thin. I "needed" to be liked by all of them, but what I *needed* was to prioritize my time. The thing that I could've said was, "I need fifteen more minutes. If that's too long, I hope you can find someone else to help." In the example of the unruly hospital visitor, what I "needed" was for the visitor to like me, but what I *needed* was physical safety, for both myself and my fellow chaplain Ericka. I was risking her safety too, after all. So instead of throwing myself and her under the bus, I could've told the visitor, "I hear you, but I also need everyone here to feel safe. Can you help us with that part?"

If you end up in any of those cases, you can still be cut off, thrown out, given a mean look. Advocating for your needs can be a lonely gig. Even at your best, some people won't like you. Even if you did everything to control someone's opinion of you, they might reject you anyway. It's a bad feeling. You can boldly say the thing you want to say, but you won't get your needs heard all the time. Not fully, not on this side of things.

I believe, really, that only God can meet our needs. Who else could, anyway? If that's true, and I'm sure it is, then nobody has enough to give or withhold that will fulfill me like it ought to. Like the psalmist said, I can say, *What can mere mortals do to me? The* LORD *is with me; he is my helper.*[15] God is the truest partner. At times, God is the only partner.

Still, my urge to cater to everyone all the time is not easy to manage. But I'm trying these days to meet people's demands without fawning all over them. I'm finding it's good to enjoy making somebody happy, instead of feeding off of it like I'm depending on it. I've learned that pleasing people is different than people-pleasing; *one is really serving and the other is serving myself a pat on the head.* I'm certain it's better that people reject the actual me and not some strange, makeshift version of myself. I've found that it's okay to be angry because it points to something truthful, to the piece of me that was lost. And I'm learning that loving people doesn't mean giving away foolishly and that boundaries and taking care of myself are a part of loving, or I can't really love at all.

A WORD FOR YOU:

Stand Up to Yourself

I taught a seminar on **self-care** recently. Besides realizing that I was also preaching to myself, the other thing I found was that most people already knew how to take a break. You already know you need a vacation or a massage or mindful breathing or a stress ball or a sword fighting class or a drawer full of chocolates. There are a million tactics like that. When you hear about self-care, it's mostly about resting and treating yourself, and that's a good thing. What I didn't know was that self-care also involves the power of saying *no.*

The power of saying, *I'm just one person.*

The power of saying, *I'm all booked right now.*

The power of saying, *You can't guilt-trip me into giving what I don't have.*

The power, even, of *saying no to yourself.*

This means knowing your limitations enough not to double-book or make grand promises or have it all done by morning. It means setting clear expectations about the kind of work you can and can't do. It means knowing when to delegate or to start sending out your résumé or to leave your phone on another planet. And yes, it means disappointing people. But if they couldn't hear your *no*, then they only wanted you for the thing you could do— and in that case, you were always right to say no.

Self-care isn't just a thing you schedule, but a way to move and be, a rhythm that allows you to give your all without giving all of yourself away.

Pastor Cho once told me: "I don't want you to work hard for the next week or the next month. Not even the next year. I want you to find a way to do this work for a lifetime." Those words saved my life.

You need a pace. You can only move as fast, or as slow, as your heartbeat will allow. Whichever way that looks for you, you might have to quit a lot of things or rearrange a lot of things or step down from something altogether. Or you might have to say the painful words, *I can't do this like I used to.*

You need a healthy tempo, because we need you. We really do.

— — —

Here are some ways to learn how to manage the voice of exalting others.

1. *Ask: What is the thing I want to say?* Or put another way, What do I need right now? Your needs are real. Your anger is real. Trace it all the way down. Suppressing your needs will only hurt you.

2. *Not everyone is going to like it when you say what you need.* But that's just fine. There are safe people and communities who will listen. They will find out what you need. They want to know how to help. Be that kind of friend too.

3. *Seriously, take care of yourself.* It's good to give yourself fully, but not to give all of yourself away. Find your rhythm of rest, but also have clear rules about your limitations. Find the power of no, especially when it comes to saying it to yourself. And while it's good to serve people, your safety can't be found in their satisfaction.

SAY EVERYTHING

The moment came like they said it would. Audrey called these moments an opportunity for growth. A screenplay might call them the Turning Point. We can decide right then to hide or grow.

Here was mine. I found myself in the strange position of having to correct a doctor.

When the doctor went to talk with a patient's family, a chaplain usually came along. It was a tag-team situation: the doctor breaks the news, the chaplain deals with how it gets broken.

We got to the waiting room and the doctor announced, "Your wife is still alive." That was only technically true. The guy's wife was being kept alive on vasopressors and machines, barely. *Her vitals are incompatible with sustaining life* is how I've heard it, a fancy way for saying there's no coming back.

I waited for the doctor to say, "But her vitals are—" and the rest, but nothing. The husband jumped up and hugged the doctor big time, just about kissed him on the neck.

In the hallway, I turned to the doctor. I opened my mouth to say something. The thing I wanted to say was, *That wasn't true and you know it.*

What came out was a squeaking noise.

I mean, the doctor was a real doctor. What did I know? Maybe it was right to give some hope. Maybe it was fine if the patient's husband found out later. Maybe it wasn't my place to say anything.

But if it were me, I'd want to know what was happening.

Then I asked the doctor, "I just want to know, how are you feeling about that conversation?" My voice shook a lot more than I wanted it to.

"Not good," he said. "Pretty bad, actually."

"Do you think there's a way we can clarify what's going on?"

He nodded quickly. And right then, I saw a nervousness in him, more than mine, because this was his everyday: being the harbinger of bad news, turning lives into before-and-after split-screens, the clinical villain in every story. He was at least as scared as I was. He needed a True Partner as much as I did.

We turned around and went back to the waiting room. The doctor immediately told the husband, "I'm sorry. I should've said this earlier. The truth is that your wife's vitals are not compatible with sustaining life."

The husband launched at us. "What does that mean, doctor? Huh? What's that mean?"

"It means she's not likely to make it."

The husband leaned over and flipped a table. No kidding, the table smacked into the window beside him. He lunged at the doctor, but a friend jumped in and held him. The friend asked us to get out.

We left fast.

"Chaplain," the doctor said.

"Doctor," I replied.

There was nothing else to say. We shook hands and parted.

— — —

In some ways, I had found it easier to advocate for the husband and for the doctor—much easier, I think, than to advocate for myself. That pointed to the problem: We say the worst things to ourselves that we'd never say to anyone else, and we root for others while forgetting to root for ourselves.

But in the husband and doctor, I saw myself too, a guy who needed a little help—so I was able to speak up for me like I had for them. It's a weird thing, I know. Weird, and true.

I had read that when we see ourselves in the third person, we have more compassion for ourselves and get a boost of bravery.[16] In other words, instead of asking, *What do I need?* it's better to say, *What does Jane need?* Instead of saying, *You can do this,* it's better to say, *John can do this.* It's like rooting for somebody in a movie, except that somebody is you. Seeing yourself in a story, it seems, gives you enough empathy to advocate for yourself the same way you'd stick your neck out for a friend.

I have often wondered how I could do such a thing. How I could find the courage to say what was true even when it was hardest. And if I saw myself from the point of view of God, the real advocate, in the same way He sees me, then I could step up for a guy like me. If you could see yourself from His side of things, you might root for yourself a bit more. You might believe you have a voice worth hearing.

CHAPTER 5

The Voice
That Condemns Others:
A Universe in My Pocket

Judgment, Resentment, and Control

*The girl gave him a look which ought to have stuck
at least four inches out of his back.*
— PHILIP MARLOWE, *THE LONG GOODBYE*[1]

I GOT A SCORE TO SETTLE

I have to tell you the truth: the chaplaincy program saved my
marriage. I'm not kidding. My wife and I had only been married
eight months and we were practically done with each other. I had
looked up divorce papers and everything.

I'm not saying that some program can save a marriage. But the program helped me realize that I wasn't beyond repair—and as a bonus, my marriage got resurrected.

What I had to figure out first was that I was a mean sort of guy. I had to get ahold of this **voice of condemning others**.

Just a few weeks into marriage, my wife and I entered into a kind of scorekeeping contest. If I met my wife's requests, I was on her good side. If I failed in any way, I was chewed out. It got to the point where she hawk-eyed me over the shoulder and waited until I slipped. My wife had a permanent eye-roll about her, eyes rolled back far enough to see 1984.

I did the same thing in another way. I measured my wife on her ability to root for me. I wanted her to encourage me constantly, like she was my cheerleader-sidekick. My constant message to her was, *Validate me, I'm doing important stuff over here.* On Sundays at church, I told her I had to ignore her so I could help these other people, *they need me, so don't get in my way.* My wife, though, just couldn't get onboard with that sort of thing. Who could? Like a kid, I went into fits about it. Why can't you make me feel like a man, an important man? I got so frustrated during one argument that I threw a bag of tomatoes at the wall. My dog didn't look at me for days. Another time I was so angry that I took about twenty ibuprofen to calm down. And another time I had such a tantrum about my wife's "obvious lack of admiration" that I fell into a catatonic state, so my wife went camping with her parents to avoid the situation.

We soon threw around the word *divorce* like confetti. But I didn't get help until a quiet moment when my wife looked at me across the dining table and said, "I don't know how to be around you." I asked, "How do you mean?" And she said, "I'm just scared to do anything you don't like. It's like I can't mess up around you."

I was devastated. She was right. I didn't know how to let her *be*.

It's a familiar story. When people don't fit our spectacular expectations, we judge them. Hatred ensues. But one of the surprising things I found out about judging people is that it's rarely about judging at all. The hatred often comes from a voice that is only a few degrees off from something good.

SOMEONE'S GETTING SAVED TODAY

I had thought that the voice of condemning others could be fixed by filtering my words and actions. If I could get ahold of my mouth and hands, if I could just quit being so judgmental, then I'd be a classy guy. And that's true some of the time. But it turns out, the problem and solution go deeper than that. Like most things, it wasn't only about the behavior. The main problem wasn't that I was a bad guy, but that I was trying to be a good one.

What I suffered from is this idea I call the Main Character Syndrome. I know the name is ridiculous, but it sounds like what it is. Main Character types see themselves as a Hero-Savior and everybody else as a secondary prop. The Main Character feels more *real* than everyone else. It's the same way that infants don't have object permanence: *if I don't see it, it doesn't exist.* In the case of adults, *I count and you don't. I matter more than you.*

This idea has been around for a while. The Jewish philosopher Martin Buber talked about it in his book *I and Thou.* When we treat somebody in an *I-It* disparity, the other is *It*, a lesser object, just a canvas we use for our own catharsis. The right way to treat somebody is in an *I-Thou* partnership, which sees them as a whole person in union with us. Buber said it like this: "Egos appear by setting themselves apart from other egos. [But] persons appear by entering into relation to other persons."[2] In other words, *I-It* denies a person's being, and *I-Thou* affirms that person's being.

I heard of a patient with a brain injury that caused her to literally believe she was the one and only protagonist in her story. She believed that when she slept, the whole world turned off, and that when she argued with people, they were only figments of her imagination. The patient lived this way with a kind of resignation—but for me, I tended to live that way with a tingling self-righteousness.

Here are a few things about Main Characters like me.

- A Main Character type is usually a Hero who has to vanquish a Villain and save a Damsel. A Villain is an obstacle to shove out of the way and a Damsel is an object for self-fulfillment.[3]

- Anyone interrupting the Main Character's story is against him and anyone aiding is for him. So if you cut him off in traffic, you're his sworn enemy.

- A Main Character also tends to think, "I'm the norm, so conform to me." Anyone outside this Puritan code is an aberration that has to be homogenized or run out of town.

- Main Characters build a self-righteous worth out of a "heroic cause." Martyrdom ("I suffer more than you") or charity ("I donate, what do you do?") are on a grading scale.

- Main Characters have a hard time with hearing no.

- Main Characters expect everyone to operate at full capacity all the time, as if everyone is a Supporting Cast at their constant beck and call.

- Main Characters often assume the worst motives in others. This is the "story you make up," says Brené Brown, a conspiracy theory that "they're out to get me."[4]

- The Main Character has an ultimate goal for everybody: conversion. And if people don't convert, then they have to be conquered.

He looked at me as if I was a cigarette stub, or an empty chair. Just something in his line of vision, without interest for him.
— PHILIP MARLOWE, *THE LONG GOODBYE*[5]

I KNOW WHAT'S BEST, KID

I really think the Main Character stuff almost killed my marriage.

This is embarrassing to say, but my wife was just a side character in the movie of my life. And as long as I saw myself as the director, the "normative baseline," I would automatically condemn her. I would pick at her choices for being "abnormal." I would tell my wife I was just trying to help her, but I was trying to carve my wife into my own image. *Listen here, I know what's best, lady.* I thought that if she just did things *my way,* that it would all work out. *Become like me,* I was saying, *and there won't be a problem.*

What I was really doing was writing my wife into a different kind of person, and by doing so, I was writing my wife out of existence. I was replacing her with some whatever-you-say robot version of herself.

If you're mad at me right about now, you have a good reason to be. I was a garish, gaudy bully. But it took me a while to get to the bottom of this because I was so certain I was the hero.

"Trying to be a hero" is not a wrong thing in and of itself. Everybody wants to be a hero for good reasons—but those good reasons can go rotten. You can sincerely fight for something, but without self-awareness, that "something" can escalate into a fatal sort of imperial manifesto.

First it starts as, *I want to fix what's wrong.* Then it moves to *Here's what I would've done.* Then it turns into crushing others who fall out of line: *You better do this or else.*

This might be a stretch, but it seems to be how most hate groups work.[6] I heard in this interview with Megan Phelps-Roper, the granddaughter of the founder of Westboro Baptist Church, that before she left the church, she believed she was doing good for the world.[7] Leah Remini, actress and former member of the Church of Scientology,[8] and Sarah Edmonson, formerly of the cult NXVIM,[9] both said the same sort of thing. Cults don't grow by saying, "Let's hate a bunch of people" (though that can definitely be part of their mantra), but instead by saying, "Let's correct what we think is wrong with everything."

My guess is that you're not in a hate group, but on an everyday level, it's possible you can condemn someone out of the grid of your own growth, or with some terms you just learned from a blog post or your therapist—none of which are bad things, but can be recklessly employed to force others into a growth spurt. Making somebody sprint that way, though, leads to busted knees and soles that bleed.

Weirdly enough, condemning others is usually an *overreach of justice*. Main Characters end up operating out of a sense of goodness as absolute. It becomes a sort of *weaponized morality* to feel accomplished and strong, all by wielding moral parameters over another person. *And it's when our values become an absolute measure of worth that we condemn each other.*

It seems Jesus said that "hate is murder" because by only accepting people who match our exact specifications of beliefs and behaviors, we are "disappearing" those who don't. We're essentially saying, "Be like me or you don't exist." Or, "I'd rather you be someone you're not." That's no better than hate, and it's crushing somebody out of existence. I've spent a lot of terrible energy doing just that, overriding somebody's point of view, forcing them into my ideology.

The silly thing is that those of us who condemn others the most probably think we're doing the most justice for the world. That's how it goes. All the triumphalist rhetoric that says "Don't listen to the haters" or "God is on *your* side" or "This world is going to hell" is conjuring up a phantom enemy, and in turn, a false sense of heroic purpose.

NO MORE MR. GOOD GUY

I talked with Josh Riebock, the author of one of my favorite books, *Heroes and Monsters.* He had some great insight about this hero and villain stuff. I asked him, "What is the biggest lie you think that people believe today?" Without hesitation he said:

> The biggest lie is, "I'm the good guy." I see that play out in religion, in politics, in finance, in marriage, in friendships, in family—that somehow, "I have to be right." The way that mindset empowers me to act negatively is so, so dangerous. If I believe I'm the good guy, if I believe I'm the hero of this story, then that creates in me this justifiable mandate to judge, tear down, draw lines in the sand, oppose, shout at, rather than asking, "Am I the good guy?" I see even in the way Jesus taught, the characters who are in the most danger in most of his stories are the ones who assume they're right. It's the older son in the prodigal son story, the priest and the Levite in the story of the Good Samaritan. On and on, they prove to be the greatest danger to the people around them. In a very archetypal way, if you believe you're the good guy, it inherently means that you're "standing for what is right," and then at no point are you going to pause and ask if your position is actually beneficial to culture at large, to anyone beyond you. But if you say, "I don't know that I'm the King Arthur in the story," that warrants pause, reflection, discussion, learning, humility. Maybe I'm not the good guy and maybe they are. And maybe I need to learn or shut up or listen or grow or evolve or repent.[10]

IF I SAVE YOU, I SAVE ME

At the bottom of this heroic purpose motive, my suspicion is that the Main Character wants to make justice in the world because there is some kind of injustice they also suffered, which festers inside. Essentially, *if I can save you, I can save me.*

I said at the start of the chapter that the voice of condemning others is just a few degrees off from something good. That's true. That voice emerged from a desperate and destructive hope to fix everything I decreed wrong. But really, I was trying to fix me. That was the big idea. *The way we try to fix others is an extension of how much we want to fix ourselves.* Like Brené Brown says, "We're hard on each other because we're using each other as a launching pad out of our own perceived shaming deficiency."[11]

This would mean that Main Character types are acting out of an internal drama, trying to save a tarnished version of themselves. That makes me more sad than angry, to recognize that we're hard on others as a reflection of how fractured we feel. I would say, in fact, that the voices of exalting others and condemning others are not so different: wanting to keep people happy and wanting to fix them are both frantic attempts at regaining safety.

By "fixing" my wife, I thought I was doing a grand service for her, but I was secretly trying to cure some kind of disorder I thought I had. When I found things to condemn in my wife, I was finding the things I hated most in myself. In "loving" her, I was hammering out a self-salvation project. And by trying to save her so much, I couldn't see the giant plank in my own eye. All along, I was Dr. Frankenstein, and I was stitching up my wife for my own ends. Tinkering with omnipotence. Playing God. Conforming others to my will. I was carving my wife into my own image to heal my own image.

I have to wonder how many politicians, bloggers, pastors, and parents have been externalizing their insecurities and trying to make "miniature versions" of themselves in a sort of redemption trophy case. When they demonize others, I wonder if they're sweating out their own demons in a public self-exorcism. I wonder how many parents are hard on their own kids because they're trying to fix some "weak" part of themselves or attempting to confer their own being into the kid as a sort of self-cloning exercise. All of us, just projecting our expectations all over the place. In the end, this sort of "fixing" is a closed circuit, fixated on itself, not really trying to help anybody else.

THE SECRET TO SWEET OLD COUPLES: OUR WILL BE DONE

Fixing others, in fact, won't fix anything, not in me or anyone else. I learned this from old people in the hospital.

I started asking elderly couples in the hospital how they made it for so long. Not how they had lived so long, but how they made it so long in marriage. The question was unprofessional, but I had to know. I asked them, "What's your secret? How did you do this? Aren't you tired?" And, "Is there hope for a guy like me?"

There were a lot of different answers, but a common thread kept popping up.

We never tried to change each other. We just let each other be.

I asked, "How can you do something like that? Aren't you worried they'll walk you down?"

Of course. That's part of the deal. If they love you, they're always sorry about the things they've done wrong. They'll change on their own. But they can't be sorry if you make them feel bad. You can't wave around "you're wrong" all the time. They'll never change then.

I mean, that's a dangerous thought. What about accountability? What if you enable somebody? But there's a difference, a big one, between accountability and demanding blood. The former aims to flourish, and the latter moves by force. There's been enough research by now that even when you hold someone accountable, it has to be done in the context of thinking the best of them, of seeing their better angles.[12]

If you try to force change in someone with shame and dirty looks, they'll change for a while, but not for very long. Your demands might be good, but a demand is only an external apparatus that adds a fresh coat of paint and a pile of scattered bricks. It never works on the inside. The people around you will comply to keep you quiet, but they won't know why.

This shouldn't be a shocking discovery. But for people like me, it was. I find it hard to be hands-off. I struggle to delegate things. I keep thinking it'll all go wrong. I judge quietly, coax loudly, breathe heavily. And when I trust people to do something, it *can* go wrong, and does. That's the learning part for them. If I swoop in to sweep up, nobody learns. They only learn to avoid messing up around me.

MARRIAGE IS A LIFELONG CROSSOVER EPISODE

My supervisor Frida told me that the next time my wife expressed a concern, to make it as important as possible.

Be a team. Not you versus her. Not her versus you. She is not the enemy. She is not better or worse. Find out how you can help. Be a team.

With all that in mind, I started tuning in. And truthfully, I was alarmed by my inability to validate my wife's wants and needs. I noticed I was always mad that she didn't say the things I thought she should say, or upset she didn't like the things I liked. I soon realized a sad thing: I tended to have the same sort of dismissal toward *everyone*. I saw my own values and passions as true and noble, but I had a hard time getting into other people's pursuits if they didn't pass my benchmark. Even in casual conversations, I noticed how much I referenced myself or replied to somebody's story with my own grand tales.

I was only seeing through my own eyes. I needed to see with more eyes than my own.

This kind of seeing is called *sonder* (the opposite of *solipsism*), the realization that everyone has a complex and vivid life of their own.[13] It can also be developed and trained. Seeing someone fully through their eyes is like learning a second language or a musical instrument and it can be done if you pause a few seconds to imagine what it's like from their side.[14] For true connection to happen, I would have to enter the room as a fellow traveler, not some pseudo-savior. For marriage or medicine or the workplace to operate without judgment, I'd have to enter with hands wide open.

When you hold your values with an open hand, you can finally begin to ask, "What is good and bad about this value? Is this value going to work for us?" Then you can toss it, keep it, or rework it. But if you hold your values with a closed fist, you get into a self-righteous waiting game, tapping feet until the other side "comes around."

Be a team. Find out how you can help. Be a team.

I had to see my wife as her own person, my patients as peers, my world as a living, breathing myriad of real voices with their own interior lives. No more sidekicks and sculptures. If I was going to be a champion, I needed to be one *for*, not over.

I had to stop trying to be the hero of the story, but *help others be the hero in theirs.*

This way is a kind of dance. A big trust. It's not hero-to-victim, but a partnership, a jazzy duet. There's a kind of presence that wants to see somebody at their best, but does that by moving *with* instead of against. It's involvement without interception, a hands-on that's mostly hands-off. It's not over the shoulder, but shoulder to shoulder. It takes longer, and it doesn't always look like it's working. But it's the only way to life and growth. It seems that when people talk about *the grace of God,* this is what they mean. Grace is the only thing that can tenderize a heart enough that the person will not only change, but *want* to change. With or without you there.

Dear God,

Today I hereby resign as general manager of the universe.

Love,

George.

—GEORGE MCCAUSLIN[15]

A WORD FOR YOU:

Somebody Has to Be You

Look, I don't think everybody's values are equal or that you can simply empathize with just anybody. No way. But the majority of the time, a relationship gets cut off too quickly. The blame gets tossed around and nobody wants to offer peace. A dinner argument turns into a bunch of slammed doors. Your workplace is blasting everybody behind their back. Your kids know *they're* right, and you know *you're* right, and everybody who isn't you is the crazy one.

I know, it's easier to keep the doors locked and the bridges burning. And in some cases, that's the right idea. If there's abuse or coercion involved, I'll be the first to bring you kerosene for the bridge. A lot of times, though, in most of our relational situations, it takes a little bit of grace and humility to repair the whole thing. And without the lightness of grace, there's a zero percent chance that the doors will open. With grace, you might get a one-percent chance. That's always been the way. It's zero or it's one. If it's going to be one, then somebody has to go first. I'm telling you that it can be you. It's you.

You can end it, you know. You can end the feud. You can condemn condemnation. You can knock on the door. You can ask how to help. You can apologize first. You can humble yourself first. You can admit you're wrong. You can extend peace. You can grieve over them instead of shouting over them. You can hold up the mirror to yourself—first.

It's hard, I know. Patience feels like losing and grace feels like pain. It will cost you to love on people. But the alternative is far worse—and it costs even more. If you look around you, you know what I mean. Hate feels like winning but it scorches the soil and starves the earth. Grace is the only seed that will bloom.

Bridges can be rebuilt, even burned ones. But somebody has to start building from their end. It starts with laying down your plank first.

— — —

I think about the thing Jesus said about planks: *Why do you look at the speck of sawdust in your brother's eye and pay no attention to the plank in your own eye?*[16] I sort of imagine a guy walking around with a two-by-four sticking out of his head, knocking over things, yelling in everybody's general direction. An online commenter, maybe. Your relatives at Thanksgiving. Your boss every Monday. And, well—me. We all have a plank problem. I suppose God could have yanked it right out of my eye. But that doesn't change anybody. I think about how Jesus had no specks, no blemishes, nothing to reproach, really, *but He took up my plank and He hung on it anyway*. When I want to judge someone, I meditate on that sort of grace. He saw me, and His love reached into the depths. That's the sort of grace that transforms a guy like me.

There's something valuable here that the gospel is offering. It fixes the wound in me that I was trying to fix in everyone else. Since I have already been healed by Christ who saw me and loved me anyway—I wouldn't run around poking at people's eyeballs, bothering them about their specks. I would probably treat their eyeballs as gently as Jesus treated mine. *To the degree to which I am no longer condemned, I no longer condemn the other person so much either.* And the gospel story removes my itchy burden of trying to be the hero because I was the one who needed rescue and the real Hero came for me. I'm glad to be the cameo in that story.

— — —

Here's how we can manage the voice of condemning others.

Value their values. Take somebody's values at face value. If it's important to them, it's important to you.

Tear up your wish list. A wish list of expectations is too easily weaponized. Besides, it doesn't work for a real person who has real needs and limits. Rip that up, and rip up the wish list of yourself, too.

Be a team. Don't assume you're the good guy, or that only you can do good. Ask, How can I help? Your story isn't yours alone. Share the pen.

— — —

On a night, dark and cold, I wrote a list of everything I wanted my wife to be and I burned it up. All my old romantic ideas up in smoke. What a selfish list it was, to think I had such a right. I had to surrender the tyranny of a self-made throne, because in a kingdom like mine, nobody had a shot. I quit the leading role and took on a walk-on. The crown and all of it: I gave it up. I found my kicks by celebrating my wife for who she is, not what she was or wasn't doing for me.

I'm not saying marriage became a smooth ride right then. But I quit trying so hard to hog the spotlight and chew up the scenery. I got off the high horse and got a two-seat carriage. I found that dancing was more beautiful when it was done in tango. It was harder maybe, but arm in arm, eyes and elbows in lockstep, we were going places.

I wish I had leaned into the dance earlier. It makes me crazy thinking about the lost time. When I got there, whole worlds opened up. What somebody else wants might not be what I want, but that's the beauty of it. Two people get together and create something they never could have on their own.

CHAPTER 6

Almost Perfect Harmony: Between Stars and Dust, I Breathe

Balancing All the Voices

And yet she was wholly herself: a rarity.
—DONNA TARTT, *THE GOLDFINCH*[1]

There's a simple thing I found out about these voices, and I hope it changes your life.

I think it's this simple, and this hard.

The four *internal* voices—self-doubt, judging, ego, and people-pleasing—have a common goal. They're driven by a singular purpose. They're each trying to heal something that wriggles underneath the surface of our guts, something that's pulsing and sliding and writhing down there.

We exalt ourselves to avoid it.

We condemn ourselves to prevent it.

We exalt others to deflect it.

We condemn others to fix it.

These internal voices mostly came about to cope with something serious. Trauma broke in and robbed you of safety. Or anxiety and depression rented a room in your head. Or loss and labels, failure and rejection, trials and injustice—they all in some way smuggled in the idea, *You're no good.* When negative voices shouted, your voices became a way to shout back. The condemnation and exaltation, of yourself and others, have been drastic counter-measures to regain solid footing. To fight the idea that you're no good.

Here's what I mean.

You might puff yourself up so you don't have to look at all the ways you've fallen short.

You might be hard on yourself because your body is telling you, *You failed really hard back there, so don't ever try that again.*

You might people-please because by latching onto a stronger person, you can vicariously live in their praise.

And you might be hard on others because by "saving" them, essentially you're saving yourself.

I think it's that simple, and that hard.

My friend explained it to me like this. Let's say you have a serious leak in your house. You call a plumber. He says he's too busy that day. You'll likely respond in one of four ways.

You can yell, "Don't you know who I am?"

Or you can whisper, "Please, I'm just a sad, small nobody."

Or you can plead, "I'll pay you double and fix you a hot meal."

Or you can shout, "Look, you're being ridiculous."

My friend told me that these kinds of interactions are Plus One and Minus One. You either have to go over the plumber or beneath the plumber. You either flex or shrink.

In the same way, there's a leak in our system, and we go Plus One or Minus One to get it patched up. Soon it becomes a way of life, and we swing wildly between extremes.

— — —

In a one-on-one, Audrey asked me, "What would it be like if you knew you were a good chaplain? If you just knew you were good?"

"Jeez," I said. "Well. If I could accept that I was *good*, it would probably fix the whole thing. Then I wouldn't be bowing down to people all the time or trying to fix others to fix me. I wouldn't judge people so much or beat myself up too hard or get too mean with anyone because—well, I'd be *too full* to do that sort of thing. I'd be my own wellspring. I wouldn't have to squeeze people to fill me up. I could enjoy my own company for once. It would fix a whole lot just to believe that I was good."

If I knew that I was *good,* and I didn't have to flex or shrink for it, then I wouldn't need to go *Plus One* or *Minus One* all the time. The problem was that I couldn't find that sort of stable and solid ground, one that wasn't over or under anyone, but simply *level,* simply *good.* I had always stolen *good* from somewhere by inflating or deflating. I had to, because on some level, I was certain that I had no good of my own.

How do we land on a solid place then?

What does that even look like?

How do we balance all these voices so they quit swinging us around?

SAY IT LIKE YOU MEAN IT

Here's how I landed. It all came to a head like this.

We were in our mid-year chaplaincy evaluations. The group time was led by Audrey. Each of the chaplains wrote an analysis of all the other chaplains in the room, and then we read it out loud to each other.

Halfway through my turn, Brady stood up.

"Stop," he told me. "Stop this right now, man."

"Stop?"

"Look, you just keep taking all the criticism. You're just … *nodding*. It's creepy. You're not challenging any of it. Not all of it can be true, right? Do you believe *all* the criticism? Can't you push back a little?"

"I'm trying to be teachable," I said. "I want to get better and everything." I almost added, *Unlike you.*

"Yeah, sure, all right," Brady said, still standing. "Enough of that. You're a good chaplain, okay? Come on. You can say that, can't you?"

"Really? You want me to say that *out loud*?"

"Yes," Brady said, sitting down. Of all things, he looked sad. "Say it like you believe it. You're a good chaplain."

I laughed. The other chaplains weren't laughing. I stopped.

"Okay," I said. "If that's what you want." I started forming the words, "I'm a good—" and would you believe it, my mouth got heavy and my stomach did a spin. I tried again. I stammered for a full minute and couldn't get the words out. All my pores opened up and I couldn't look anybody in the face. It sounds silly, but it was a very sad situation too.

Have you tried it before? It's not easy. It's difficult to affirm yourself that way. *I'm a good father. A good mother. A good doctor. A good barber. A good teacher. A good speaker. A good student. A good neighbor. A good daughter. A good son.*

Hardly anybody is comfortable with the idea. There's always some other voice that counters, *Are you sure about that? You really think so? Who are you, anyway? Is your mirror working? Are you wearing pants right now?*

"Well," I finally said. "I heard a long time ago from somebody that I wasn't so bad."

"That's not what Brady asked," Audrey said. "Can *you* say you're a good chaplain? Do *you* believe you're a good chaplain?"

I pulled out two sheets of paper from my wallet.

"This list here," I said, holding up the first paper, "is a list of good things that people have told me about myself. And this other list," I said, holding up the other one, "is a list of all the bad things that people told me. The bad list is a lot longer. I carry these two lists around with me all the time. Most days, it's hard to know which list to believe. So no, I don't know if I *can* say that I'm good. I don't know that."

I set the lists down. No one rushed in to say anything. No counter-flood of praise. Like the training taught us, they let me soak in the moment.

Then Brady spoke up. He said, "There's this Jewish tradition with rabbis where they carry around two pieces of paper, one in each pocket. One piece of paper says, *I am but dust and ashes.* And the other one says, *But for my sake the world was created.*"

Brady stood up and walked over to me. I remembered the last time he had done that, it didn't go over so well. But this time, he kneeled down and put a hand on my shoulder. He took a long look at me, eyes welling, very earnest. "The bad news is that you're dust and ashes, sure, but *a whole planet was made for you.* That's some good news, isn't it?" He was really tearing up now. "You got a long way to go, chap. I know I do, too. But you're good. I wish you'd believe that. You're worth a planet. You're really all right."

"Thank you, Brady," I said. "I think that's my favorite thing I've ever heard you say."

We shook on it.

THE ONES WHO STICK AROUND A WHILE

Trying to balance the tension between the bad list and the good list, of being both dust and planets, is not an easy thing to do. But I believe that balance is possible, and crucial, for a solid kind of identity.[2]

I think of it like this. When I was in the dating scene, I was anxious all the time because one wrong move could make a girl get up and go. I couldn't show the weird parts of me, no blemishes or anything like that. Dating was a shifty game of constantly marketing my own merchandise. I mean, this is how it goes. Nobody is "owed" anything in the dating world. But the game was nerve-racking. I was a salesman, see. Give me a shot, will you, and I'll make all your dreams come true. Just don't look too close; this dream is a low resolution screenshot.

When I got married, I didn't have to sell those dreams anymore. My wife was in for good, in for the reality of two people making it work. I had some assurance that my wife would stick around if I messed up. I could tell her, "Look, you signed this marriage license and there were witnesses." But the assurance didn't come from the paper she signed. She had vowed to stay. So I didn't have to hide; she saw me naked, in full daylight and everything. She accepted me, as much as she could anyway, for the kind of guy that I was. She learned, and I did too, that even our worst stuff was a story about something we needed.

In all that was a glimpse of divine acceptance, the kind that would help me to accept the parts of me that I hadn't before.

— — —

I've seen that kind of love in the hospital. The type of love that I've seen in a patient's room is the closest I've ever seen to God's sort of love.

Occasionally a patient is so unsettled by their own condition that they don't want any visitors at all. They're scared of how they look to everyone. If you've ever been a hospital patient, you know what I mean. You're disheveled, you start to stink a bit, your orifices are singing off key. I'd want privacy too. I don't want anybody to see that stuff—my bad list.

The hardest thing is when a patient's friend sees the patient and runs for the exit. It happens, and I can't judge that. Seeing illness is startling, and it's not the way you see it in a well-lit TV drama. Seeing your loved ones oozing from a hundred places is incomprehensible. And no friend or family member can be expected to jump in heroically and drain themselves empty.

Still, that first reaction, the hesitation, the flinch, the wide eyes: it's hard on a patient. If a patient with chronic illness could sum up their entire worth in a single word, usually that word is *embarrassed.* Do you know the kind of embarrassment I'm talking about? That sort of red-faced, stomach-sick humiliation? It's what the French call *malheur,* a shame around pain.[3] That's what many patients feel, all the time. They believe their body's betrayal is entirely their own fault.

The story of their lives is that their illness is making them worthless—no good list, and nothing but the bad list.

But I've seen patients who open their doors and they have somebody who stays. It's the kind of love that moves through sickness and doesn't get sick of it. The sort of love that sees all the gross parts of somebody and sticks around. There's something sacred about a person moving through their loved one's slop and slobber, crinkling their noses but moving in anyway, saying, *I'm here. As long as you need me, I am here.*

Every sick patient is a stranger in their own body, horrified at the endless capacity of their own cells to turn on them, and yet grace moves in to say, *You are no stranger to me.* I've seen that sort of love, through gowns and gloves and masks and needles and diagnoses day after day. I've seen love sleeping on vinyl recliners and pacing outside of the OR and in the NICU holding their premature newborn's hand through a plastic box. I've seen spouses at bedside cleaning their wife's colostomy bags or hand-feeding their husband who doesn't remember them anymore. I've seen patients who light up at the sight of their family walking in, their own shame replaced by comfort and relief because their family loves them through all the colorful things that our bodies do when they're broken. And I've seen love when a dying woman asked her son, "Was I good? I'm so sorry, was I any good?"—and her son answered, *You were good, mom. I promise you were good. I love you, and you are the best mom in the universe.*

In some ways, I suppose it's easier to move through somebody's sickness because it's not their fault. But for that very sick part of me, what God calls *sin*, I'm at least a little bit to blame. There's no doubt I've done a ton of selfish things, enough to have kept people far and away. If people saw my *sick*, the disease in my heart, they would leave.

At the center of the story of the gospel, I imagine that my body is a house rotted by the sick, by *sin*, and by the violence of a world that has worn me down—and God walked in, over rusty nails and splintered boards, put me back together, and handed the house back to me as a gift even more beautiful than it was before. In the gospel story, the only way to heal me was that He had to absorb those nails and boards. He took my bad list into both His hands, and handed me His goodness. Intersecting with the cross, there's this gift of resurrection, an invitation into restored life for a heart as flawed and fatal as mine, and it shows me that God is in the business of breathing life into busted places. I imagine that God moves into the labyrinth of my selfishness and trauma and tragedy and history, the things that are both my fault and not mine at all, and painfully but gently navigates the gross and slippery shadows of my insides. There He says, *With you I am well pleased.* That divine voice makes its home in me. A heart as flawed and fatal as mine is still loved and all right.

This is no small thing. To be called good, to be loved, often has to be earned. It costs something. For others to move into your orbit, pour into you, dream with you, drown with you, to take on your stuff—that sort of divine love, *grace,* has a cost. But Christ has paid that already. That's what the cross was for. He poured out at the entire cost of Himself. He doesn't make you earn your way in. He moves toward you when nothing is good about you, when there's seemingly nothing to love. Like Saint Augustine said, "Quia amasti me, fecisti me amabilem," or, "In loving me, you made me lovable." Or C. S. Lewis: "He loved us not because we were lovable, but because He is Love."[4]

I'm reminded of when my wife and I first started dating. I gave her a Top Ten List of my worst shortcomings. Really. And she threw it out. She didn't ignore them; I was held accountable, sure. But by moving in with grace, those bad parts of me got healed.

It's what Christ does, too, on a wild, extravagant scale. You don't have to do a thing to achieve it. It's a matter of faith. Of receiving grace. We welcome and embrace and believe that the rumor is true: *I am called good by the most good.*

I think that's the gospel story, as best as I can tell it. That sort of love is humbling and healing, enough to galvanize you into something better. Some days I can hardly stand such a grace that sees me and lives there anyway.

I have seen it with my own eyes, and I believe.

A WORD FOR YOU:

You're a Whole Lot of Stars and Dust

What I've come to understand in light of the gospel story is that when I'm hard on myself, some of that is overblown and unfair, but some of it's true because it touches on the flawed nature of who I am. I'm dust, ashes. There's ugly stuff I need to work on. If somebody points that out—well, they don't know the half of it. When I flex real hard, some of that is from pride and arrogance, but some of it's also true because I'm valued beyond anything I could achieve. A world was made for the likes of me. I have galaxies pumping through my veins. I was made on purpose, even. If somebody throws me a compliment—well, they don't know the half of that, either.

I used to think I had to chop some off the top and some off the bottom. You know. Don't get too high or too low, find the middle ground. But it means more that I'm worth a planet *because* I'm dust and ashes. And I can handle being dust and ashes *because* I'm worth a world. Somehow, I'm Plus One and Minus One at the same time, not in a middle-of-the-road sort of way, but into a type of audacity and modesty that creates a person who is full without being full of themselves.

The same is true if we could see our neighbor the same way. If they're dust and planets, then nobody gets demonized or deified. They get dignified. C. H. Spurgeon said it like this: "He who grows in grace remembers that he is but dust, and he therefore does not expect his fellow Christians to be anything more; he overlooks ten thousand of their faults, because he knows his God overlooks twenty thousand in his own case."[5] More than that, when I exalt someone, it can get weird if I'm latching onto them, but to serve them is part of what I'm made for. And when I condemn someone, it's usually done with a harmful superiority, but it's also because I want to see the best in them, the best that God has dreamed for that person's future.

These internal voices, in some way, tap into the reality of our human condition, the fact that we're survivors trudging through sinful territory, and that sinfulness has made its way deep in us. But our voices also tap into the *Imago Dei,* that we're crafted in God's image, and so God's voice is always calling us to return to ourselves, to understand that though we are fractured and frayed, we are called into the inalterable goodness of God, and in His voice is the paradoxical truth about us: that we are infinitesimal dust yet infinitely valuable.

I am but dust and ashes—but for my sake, the world was created. Or Scripture says it this way: "For he chose us in him before the creation of the world to be holy and blameless in his sight . . . In him we have redemption through his blood, the forgiveness of sins, in accordance with the riches of God's grace that he lavished on us."[6]

All along, your voices hinted at the real rescue that was already done for you. They had a hunch, an intuition, about the True Story of the world. When you believe that rescue story, then the voices no longer have to save, but just point the way. They get unscrambled into pristine audio, reminding you both of what you need and what you already have.

You'll get a lot of negative messages over a lifetime, but a lot of that is just touching on your humanity. Your liabilities, your limitations. That you're just a person. You don't have to fear it. You could learn a lot from it, really. You'll get a lot of positive messages over a lifetime too, but that isn't much compared to being called *good* through a goodness not your own, through the very author of goodness. That's permanent. It's not something you have to pay for, but it's been paid for.

There it is. I'm dust. I'm a whole planet. Both have to be true.

If we break it down, the gospel story transforms our voices like this:

Self-exaltation is a result of covering your perceived weaknesses, *but it tells you that you rightly long to be affirmed, valued, and validated*. You get real **self-acceptance**, where you can celebrate your strengths without using them as a shield.

Self-condemnation is a result of falling short of a perfect ideal, *but it gives you an accurate view of your very human limitations*. You get real **self-awareness**, where you can hold yourself accountable without crushing yourself under an impossible version of you.

Exalting others always puts yourself too low and others too high, *but tells you that it's good to please others and to share in their satisfaction*. You get the ballast to **serve others** without absorbing identity and esteem from them.

Condemning others always tries to fix people with overcorrection, *but tells you that it's good to look out for your neighbor, especially if they are on a harmful path*. You get the grounding to **challenge others** without making them into somebody like you, to even forgive them and trust them over to God if they choose a fatal road.

SOMETIMES YOU BOMB

I guest-preached at a church recently and I bombed. It took about thirty seconds to know I was going nowhere.

I had the usual voices in my head.

That made no sense.

They're cringing bad.

Why did you say it like that?

What if your best is over?

What if this is it?

Are you wearing pants right now?

I couldn't stop sweating up there. I think the crowd was sweating for me. It was that nervous sweating when you don't know if the singer is going to hit another bad note—it's already a train wreck and you're waiting for it to hurry up out of your life—and I rushed to a merciful ending. Put the sermon out of its misery.

After I sat down, I had a moment to myself while the service was finishing. On that chair, I acknowledged I had bombed. I knew I wouldn't be invited back. I had done a lousy job, and there was no way around that.

In a notepad, I jotted down where the sermon went wrong. I also jotted down what worked, what was pretty good, in fact. I reminded myself that even though I didn't do okay, I was still okay. I could live to preach another day.

During lunch, my wife said to me, "So. Well. That wasn't good."

"I know," I said. "I'm going to take a shower for forty minutes."

"It's okay," she said. "*You're* good. You're a good chaplain." She really meant it.

"Okay," I said. "Okay. I'll take it."

PART 2

External Voices

External Voices

The first four voices, in a lot of ways, are a familiar cast of characters. Self-doubt, judging, ego, and people-pleasing are all an ancient rogue gallery, with particular tics and tricks. They can be managed by deducing their origin story and by hearing what they're trying to say. They're mostly good voices gone bad. Once you figure them out, you can usher them toward a better story. It's not simple, but it's possible. Lucky for us, the internal voices are mostly predictable and universal.

But the **next four voices—trauma, guilt, grief, and family dynamics**—are shapeshifters. They're molded by our individual stories, so they're as varied as we are, topographies in shadow, maps buried. These external voices are also harmful most of the time, with apparently little to redeem. I saw this with my patients. The past could blast in and topple them over with guilt. Their trauma was an alien virus, crawling through their tongues and fingers. The family would walk in and bust a fuse. Or the patient's grief was an unspoken vacuum, covered in smiles, just brimming at the edge of their eyes.

When we dug into all this in the chaplaincy program, I learned that my patients and I had been dealing with these voices in a lot of destructive ways. Grief and trauma, especially, had a lot of myths revolving around them that only deepened the pit and waxed the walls. The only tool I had was a shovel, not for digging deep, but digging myself under. I was up against Moriarty. Up against Goliath. Up against a wall, even. But I was determined, for my patients and myself, to uncover the mystery.

— — —

The four-quadrant model below shows *pain and loss from* self and others. While the first four voices are *valuations,* by which we grade ourselves and others, these four voices are *precipitations.* They fall out of the sky. They emerge from events, either from our surroundings or situations, most of which we don't choose at all. They're largely outside-in and seemingly inescapable.

EXTERNAL VOICES: PRECIPITATIONS

	SELF	OTHERS
PAIN FROM	**GUILT:** What I Did	**FAMILY DYNAMICS:** What I Grew Up With
LOSS FROM	**TRAUMA:** What Was Done to Me	**GRIEF:** What I Lost

First we'll look at *guilt* and *trauma,* which seem unrelated but are a package deal. Then we'll look at *family dynamics* through the story of a patient and see what parts of our family's voices can be kept or discarded. Finally, we'll look at *grief,* and how there's a better way than just "letting go."

The good news. A lot of good work has been done to get through the voices of trauma, guilt, grief, and family. We're not without help and resources. And you might find that we're not entirely strangers on this leg of the journey. You'll find some overlap like I did in our shared pains and losses. If by the end of this part of the book, your only thought is, *I knew I wasn't alone,* that will have been good enough for me. Maybe for both of us.

CHAPTER 7

Navigating Guilt and Trauma: Absolving Voices

The Things We've Done and the Things Done to Us

I guess a scar isn't so bad.
Not if it's only on one side.
I can always go through life sideways.
—DEBBY MARSH, *THE BIG HEAT*[1]

ON THE LAM, I TELL YOU

"I'm a guy on the lam trying to start fresh," I said, "and I operate out of the **voice of guilt** from all the things I had done before."

Audrey had asked me the counselor's question: *Where is all this coming from?* She was talking about my general demeanor, the way I seemed to keep my eyes low in every room, how I got twisted up when I made a mistake. I kept giving her the usual answers: my "self-doubt stuff" and my "people-pleasing thing." I could've stuck with that alibi. It fit the facts. It was partially true, anyway. But Audrey knew better. She kept digging, and finally she got it out of me.

"I'm going to tell you stuff about me that will probably make you judge me," I said. "Maybe you won't, but I'm afraid you will. Before, in my *old life,* I hurt a lot of people. I wasted a lot of time. Theirs and mine. I was an idiot: drunk every weekend in high school, running from police, going to church hung over. I've knocked out people in fights. I've shoplifted. I had these tantrums, always punching walls. I was a casual liar, a real verbal magician. I threw people under the bus, all the while convincing them they were the ones driving. I lost a scholarship because I partied too hard. Then my mom paid my way through college— but for what? She wanted me to be a doctor. It's all she asked for. I cheated her dreams. I got fired from a church. I mean, how does *that* happen? There's a lot more I shouldn't say. If people from back then knew I was a chaplain now, they'd laugh.

"My self-doubt and everything—some of that's because when I do something good, I have to wonder if it's really me or I'm just pretending to be a saint. For atonement. I second-guess myself because I can hear those people from the past in my head saying, *'I know who you are. You're not fooling me. You're scum, a no-good, low-class bum.'* And they would be right. I'm not a victim. I know what I've done. Any time I walk in a room to counsel someone, any number of people from the past can walk in and remind me of something awful I did. Their voices rush in and I freeze up. *I live in this constant state of apology.* I mean, don't I deserve to keep my head hanging in shame? Is there hope for people like me?"

— — —

We were silent for a while. Always the dramatic silence with these chaplains.

"I don't know who you were before," Audrey said. "It's hard for me to imagine you as that guy, actually. But like you said, you did those things. You felt guilty because you were guilty. You still have to hold yourself accountable, but you can't go through life with your eyes to the ground. I think you need to say goodbye."

"To my old self?"

"No," Audrey said. "Your old self is dead. You need to say good-bye to your debt."

I thought about that. What it would look like to say *goodbye* to the big idea that I owed everybody. And for some reason I felt fear. I was afraid that I was getting away with something. The debt was my way of letting the universe have its justice.

But I knew as long as I was hosting guilt, letting all my past stay in my head, I would never do anything for the right reasons. I'd let guilt push me beyond my own resources. I'd forfeit my own well-being, and then I was no good to anyone—most especially myself.

"Here's a thought," Audrey continued. "You've shared now that a lot has happened to you. What if these forces of *trauma* pushed you in a certain direction? I don't mean that you're not accountable. *But what if you were never in a place to fully live into yourself until now?*"

FATHER, FORGIVE ME
FOR WHAT I'M ABOUT TO TELL YOU

I have to pause here and tell you about Edward.

Edward was in his nineties and wanted a blessing before he died. He took one look at me and grabbed my shirt with both hands. He pulled me up close and I could hear the gurgling in his lungs.

"Forgive me," he said. I heard the lip sounds, that dry smacking noise they get in the hospital when the body rejects water. He smelled like old shoes and bleach. He also had a look about him, a sheer terror.

I asked, "What did you need forgiveness for?"

"Chaplain," he said, "are you Korean? Japanese? Vietnamese?"

"I'm—"

"Chaplain, I need you to forgive me. I need you to absolve me. I did something horrible. I did something to your people."

My stomach went funny. I threw his hands off me and took a step back.

"Please?" he said, trying to grab me again. "Please." His eyes shook in his head. "What I did to them . . . I can't stop hearing their voices."

I took another step back. "I can't," I said. "I can't do that for you."

I ran from the room. I stumbled to an elevator. The lights inside were broken and I went down eight floors in darkness. *Which people? What did he do? Why?*

He needed absolution. But I couldn't do it.

Edward died later that week. Alone.

— — —

I still think about him. Edward the guilty dying man. I tried looking him up. He might have been in the Korean War, or Vietnam, or the LA riots. He might have shot a soldier or civilian or a store owner. I never found out. I'm not sure I wanted to.

The voices in his head must have been unbearable. His voice, and theirs.

If I could go back, I would've tried to see him again. *I'd want forgiveness too.* That's the thing that keeps me up sometimes. I'd want a second chance, for someone to hear my regret, to know that I was truly sorry.

If I was a swell guy and I would've listened longer, I probably would've heard that Edward was just a kid when he did what he did. He would've barely comprehended the craziness of the world around him. A kid in a war, a riot, in survival mode, scratching his way through wilderness: what could he have done differently, anyway? I mean, nothing would justify the pain he had caused. But I want to believe he had been in a horrific situation with limited options. That his entire environment was fraught with chronic, retaliatory violence without a hint of relief. In a place like that, a guy like him could only become the worst version of himself—a version even he was disgusted by.

What if he never had a place to fully live into himself?

That's the story I'd like to make up for Edward. But I was finding, over and over, that I didn't have to make up that story very much. His story, like mine, was just about everybody else's story too.

OUT OF THE PAST: A WORLD OF TROUBLE

*When your head says one thing
and your whole life says another,
your head always loses.*
— FRANK MCCLOUD, KEY LARGO[2]

A neuropsychologist taught one of our didactics on **trauma**. Trauma, she said, is a negative experience that disturbs and debilitates. Or as I heard it, *trauma is when what happens to you outweighs your ability to cope with it.* That can be anything from job loss to a break-up to physical abuse to a hurricane to a car accident. Trauma has a way of saying, *Nothing is safe anymore. It can happen again. It happened because of you.*

Trauma sounds like it has to be a "big event," but there are also the things that everyone dismisses, like words that cause intense pain or a general neglect from people you trusted. I have a friend who told me that in sixth grade, she had a hard time keeping her desk clean, and one day all the contents of her desk were all over the floor. Her teacher had done it to punish her. She was berated in front of her class: *You will never go to college and succeed at life because you're so disorganized.* My friend told me, "The adult me has never forgotten the sting and embarrassment of feeling like I just can't get organized and get it together."

That sort of thing has a way of staying with us. More than we think.

In the didactic, we learned that childhood trauma can predict certain health problems. The psychologist showed us an ACE Test.[3] ACE stands for Adverse Childhood Experiences. The test has ten questions about what happened to you before you were an adult. One version of the test asks, *"Did a parent or other adult in the household often swear at you, insult you, put you down, or humiliate you?"* and, *"Did you often feel that you didn't have enough to eat, had to wear dirty clothes, and had no one to protect you?"* and, *"Was your mother or stepmother often pushed, grabbed, slapped, or had something thrown at her? Or kicked, bitten, hit with a fist, or hit with something hard?"*[4]

If you answer "yes" to four or more of the questions, you have a higher risk for all kinds of problems. For example, your risk of depression increases by almost 500 percent and your risk of suicide goes up over 1,000 percent.[5] You're more likely to get cancer, heart disease, become an addict, or become morbidly obese—even if you don't drink or smoke or overeat.[6] You can become more prone to violence, self-harm, promiscuity, bone fractures, hepatitis, COPD, unhealthy attachments, paranoia, and cognitive difficulties. Trauma can also affect how you regulate your emotions, so you take more risks and act out a lot more.[7]

What this means is that if you've had trauma, it doesn't pass through your system like waste; it stays in your veins. Psychiatrist Bessel van der Kolk writes, "traumatized people chronically feel unsafe inside their bodies: The past is alive in the form of gnawing interior discomfort."[8] Trauma has its own voice, and it speaks when you don't want it to.

On the ACE test, I scored a nine out of ten. Basically, I never had a chance.

YOUR SCAR SAYS OTHERWISE

I never knew that the things that happened to me were not normal.

I thought every kid grew up the way that I did, with all the regular drama and hysterics. It had made me a tough guy, I would say. A real contender. I could wear my past like a badge of credibility.

But it was months into hospital chaplaincy when one of the supervisors looked me dead in the face and said, "What happened to you was not okay. You know that, don't you?"

No, I said, *I didn't know that.* I'm not sure I *wanted* to know. The thought was too much to bear.

I found out my badge was baggage: there was some serious trauma that took on a life of its own, formed its own ideas—and it had a lot to say. None of it good. I should have known these things, but you hear about those people who have lived for years with mold or radiation or a gas leak in their house, and they coughed or saw a ghost or something—but they never gave it a second thought. They learned to tolerate all kinds of demons.

— — —

I always had this feeling that my skin was loose. Porous. Like anything could get in or out. Like I was Swiss cheese, and more Swiss than cheese. All my movements were underwater, carried by the current, provoked by the latest, loudest voice. I was a guy with no muscles. My soul could barely close a fist. No strength. No compass. Just drifting, pushed along. At the same time, my soul would aggressively stretch toward people and situations that continually harmed me. I could pursue an obsession with undeterred fervor. If I liked a girl, I thought of nothing else. If I took a sip of alcohol, I'd wake up the next day in time for dinner. I was impulsive, my fuse always lit. I burned out just as fast. I'd skip classes and job interviews. I'd procrastinate out of a fear of failure. Or because I wanted to catch the next episode of a binge watch. I'd get in my car and drive for hours, miles of darkened road, seeing if I could really run away this time. I had grand plans scribbled on the back of unpaid bills. I was afraid to check voicemails and emails. My brain was always on fire. Other times it was cold, asleep. I'd get sad for days and weeks and months, crying uncontrollably, haunted by a general sense of dread. I always took up a dare, even when they tried to take it back. There are entire seasons I can't recall because I drank them away. And then there are other memories that I can't get out of my head, a permanent throb at the edge of my temples.

THE BRAIN IS YOUR SOUL-BOX

I have read tons of studies that say self-doubt, people-pleasing, and narcissism are all correlated with severe trauma. Even though I've spent a lot of time talking about how we can transcend voices like self-doubt and ego, and I believe we can—this assumes a fair playing field in which our brains are working on an even ground. It assumes "money in the bank." A traumatized brain starts from a negative balance. Trauma, whether "big" or "small," has a way of hijacking the brain so that the operations are turbulent, in disarray. If our brains are computers, then trauma is a virus, corrupting the wires and wares, so that even the very operations by which it could reprogram itself are busted.

Many of us were shaped by events against our will. This is not entirely a matter of virtue or morality. We have tried our hardest to be "good," but our ankles were tied in knots. We started a lap behind. We were no good from go.

I need to tell you: I don't mean to take away from what I did. I did hurt people. I did make terrible choices. I've suffered the consequences for that, and I believe rightly so. Trauma doesn't remove accountability. It doesn't excuse a thing. I feel guilt over the ways I've harmed others, and I should. I've seen countless abuse victims come in through the ER, and I'm on the victim's side. I know that very often, the abuser has also been abused, but that never makes it okay. I'm not about to explain that away. I'm not going to sympathize with the devil. I'm responsible for the ways I've harmed others, and you are, too—and we have to clean that up.

But I have to wonder if trauma pre-wrote some of my script and shaped my story without my consent. It seems that many of us who made poor choices were set on that path long ago. We had been stuffed with time-bombs. Trauma was a prophecy, a cruel fate, an iron web woven by Atropos.

~ ~ ~

There is this infamous study about kids and marshmallows. A kid is given a marshmallow and told that if he waits a few minutes, he'll be given a few more. But if he eats the one in front of him, he just gets the one. The study predicted that the hasty kids would grow up to be impulsive risk-takers. Some thirty years later, the kids who waited turned out to be more successful than those who didn't.[9]

The study was a big one about delayed gratification and self-control. But it was an old study done with less than a hundred kids. It was done again, this time with nearly a thousand children. The researchers noticed something new. The kids who came from high income families were able to wait, but the kids who came from low income families usually did not.[10] The possible conclusion was that *children from poor families didn't know where their next meal was coming from, so they felt like they had to eat what was available.* Their traumatic situations influenced their choices. These kids weren't bad kids. They were acting out of fear and scarcity.

Somebody with poor social skills, who melts down in conflict, and who seems to lie all the time might really be a bad guy. Or, that person *might* be someone who has had to endure their own life for a lifetime. It's possible that their trauma has put them into a hypervigilance, a perpetual fight mode, where they feel like something is out to get them around every corner.

I've always liked C. S. Lewis's take on this. He writes that somebody who appears to be a good citizen might have gotten lucky with their *raw material,* due to their "good heredity and a good upbringing" or even "good digestion," but could have easily become "a fiend" if the opposite had been true.[11] If each of us switched our situations, I might have made the choices you did, and you might have made the choices that I did. We're accountable to those choices. But there are a lot of uncontrollable forces that get us there.

If you think this is all too nice and neat, well, I think so too. I also know that without acknowledging that trauma is in the mix, we don't have much of a path forward. All we can do is blame people, or tell them, "Just make better choices." That isn't very helpful. And in that sort of world, there are no second chances for people like you and me.

SOMETHING FROM THE PAST THIS WAY COMES

There are studies that say the children of Holocaust survivors carry traumatized DNA.[12] In other words, though the children haven't been through the Holocaust themselves, the evidence shows they inherited it in their blood.[13] The same is true for anyone who descended from slaves, prisoners, criminals, or disaster survivors. While there's debate about whether the trauma is physically inherited or it's the narrative that's passed down, the legacy of trauma carries on, either through blood or bedtime stories. The question then is that if trauma comes from seemingly everywhere, is there a way to break free?

In a PBS interview, a journalist asked Rachel Yehuda, one of the researchers who looked into the Holocaust DNA: "If you're the child of a parent who experienced trauma, are you doomed to be depressed or stressed for the rest of your life?"[14]

Yehuda replied, "I don't think you're doomed, but I think that many children of traumatized parents have struggled with depression and anxiety—and many of them have felt *relieved* that there might be a contributing factor."

That's the key thing: *The way through the effects of trauma first requires getting to know that trauma has happened.* Or as van der Kolk writes, "Sensing, naming, and identifying what is going on inside is the first step to recovery."[15]

Finding out that my lifelong depression, that my broken brain and my lack of control and my days spent in a fog, could have been the result of outside forces, is sort of disheartening. But really, it's also a relief. *It wasn't entirely my fault.* So I could see this one of two ways. One was thinking that I was marked for life, permanently sideways, relegated to a shadow-life in the gutter. The other was thinking, *Finally I have an explanation for some of the mess I got mixed up in.* And if I could identify why I was here, then maybe I could find a way through.

— — —

In the chaplain's training on trauma, I asked the neuropsychologist the same sort of question:

"Is it too late for me then? Am I just doomed to a life of depression and anxiety and five hundred percent heart attacks?"

"No," she said. She mentioned the thing about first recognizing the trauma. Then she added, "There is a way through called **resilience**."

We learned that even if someone scored a nine out of ten on the ACE test, they could cope well enough if they learned some resiliency skills. A person with, say, a two out of ten still might have a difficult time because they never learned those skills. Some of the skills were *personal strategies* like meditation, relaxation, self-affirmation, highlighting a positive strength, a new belief in positive outcomes, renewed life purpose, and belief in a higher power. There were also relational skills like making *interdependent connections* and *healthy attachments.*

The good news is that just as trauma is passed down, *a better story* can be passed down, too. Renovation is possible.

A THING LIKE THAT

I also work at a nonprofit where I serve the homeless, and I met a man named Ray who had finally secured housing and landed a new job. He had told us he needed a new tool belt. He was borrowing an old one, which was falling apart. A coworker's friend heard about the situation and bought an expensive tool belt for Ray. A fifteen-pocket leather carpenter pouch, one of the nicest ones you could buy. Ray was beside himself. I mean really, he was moved. A few weeks later, somebody asked Ray how he liked the tool belt.

"I haven't used it," Ray said. "I'm not sure that I can."

Ray explained, "I don't deserve a thing like that." He didn't want to ruin it somehow. He didn't mean that he would ruin it by using it; he meant he would ruin it with *himself.* "The things I've done," he said, "pretty much disqualify me. I feel guilty."

Ray had told us his story before. It was a similar story with many of our clients, filled with abuse, abandonment, addictions, crime, an entire racket. It left him broke and homeless: a fate he felt he deserved. But eventually, Ray learned to believe a better story about himself. He learned that he didn't need to be good enough for the gift; the gift was good enough for him. The things he had done and the things that happened to him didn't disqualify him from what was good. The tool belt, in some small way, was part of changing him. Maybe Ray really was the kind of guy who didn't deserve it. But that was the point. It was a gift. We need that sort of grace, a grace that invites us into a better story about who we are, a better story than the one we were given.

At the nonprofit, one of our most emphasized values is a *trauma-informed perspective.* We receive every person in need with the idea that they're coming in on the worst day of their lives. Instead of asking, *What's wrong with you?* we ask, *What happened to you?*[16] Instead of seeing them as wrong or immoral, we first see them as injured. We try to maintain the same ethos around co-workers. If we see somebody acting out, we don't throw around accusations; we go into discovery mode.

I know that sounds a bit idealistic. And no kidding, the trauma-informed stuff is not easy. But I feel the difference: the way we move slowly, respect each other's reasons, how we believe the best about people. We trust that a person is acting a certain way because it's rooted in an event, not in ill intentions. Even if they *are* acting from ill intentions, it's still better to find out *why* instead of flinging unsavory labels.

Everybody, I believe, is injured in some way. We're all wearing casts. When somebody is wearing a cast, we navigate around it as gently as we can. If they can't run so fast, we don't tell them to hurry up. We move at their pace.

Has anybody done that for you? It's an incredible thing. If anyone has ever asked you, *What happened to you?* instead of, *What is wrong with you?*—you realize how rare it is that anyone has slowed down to understand you. You realize that everybody has been hard on you for things nobody understood, including yourself. You have the power to pause, too. You can be the one who hears the pain of another and doesn't flinch. You can choose to ask, *What happened to you?*

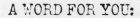

A WORD FOR YOU:

You Can Change the Score

What I've found is that there are at least five things you can do to find resilience in trauma.[17]

1. *Disclosure: Go and tell it.* I will always recommend therapy. A therapeutic alliance is one of the safest ways to talk about your stuff.[18] Whether with a therapist, safe person, or supportive group, your voice of trauma needs to be spoken aloud.[19]

2. *Social support: Find people who root for you.* Finding even one caring mentor figure makes all the difference in your recovery.[20] In a study of over 6,000 people, the marks of resilience-building include at least two non-parent adults during childhood who take a genuine interest in you.[21] I would imagine it is necessary in any stage of life to have older adults around who root for you. It's also a good idea to draw boundaries with people who don't understand yet.

3. *Self-aware strategies:* Mind your muscles, your muscles have a mind. Part of resilience is to befriend your own body again. Van der Kolk writes, "Our sense of agency, how much we feel in control, is defined by our relationship with our bodies and its rhythms . . . In order to find our voice, we have to be in our bodies—able to

breathe fully and able to access our inner sensations."[22] Skills like meditation, journaling, martial arts, dance, acting, music, prayer, and yoga are all ways to know our own bodies while mastering them—plus, the exercise helps.[23] The mastery of these skills, especially ones that move your arms and legs around, can build interoception, the ability to listen to your own body. Building up interoception can help process and interpret past trauma, while also making plans for future trauma.[24]

4. *Safe experiences: Write something new.* You need new stories to tell. Within your limits, set new goals, take a trip, and enter conversations. Find any task or hobby that has a predictable and pleasant outcome. This allows you to get back some autonomy amidst an uncontrollable situation. Your past might be set in stone, but you can still sculpt what's ahead.[25]

5. *Renewed belief: Own your story.* You also need a better story to believe.[26] When trauma occurs, it will shake up your idea of what is good and fair. But if you're able to stretch your worldview and incorporate the traumatic event into it, you have a better chance of recovery.[27] That usually means believing two contradictory things at once, such as:

   - The world is pretty good, but it can also be very dangerous.
   - That tragedy felt random and haphazard, but life still has a purpose.

- I feel guilty that I made some bad choices, but I'm sorry and I will make better ones.
- When nothing else is good, God is the only one who is.

A SLIMY, NO-GOOD SWINDLER:
YOU'VE GOT A LOT OF GUTS COMING HERE

I still wonder:

Do we ever really outlive our past?

Is it doomed to haunt us?

The guilt, the trauma, the consequences, the awful shame of it: is it my fault? The fault of a failed system? My flesh or a flawed world? Both?

I was at this dinner party one time where I was trying to make an impression, and someone from my past showed up. Immediately, he began to tell stories about me to the circle around us.

He couldn't believe that a guy like me, with split knuckles and quick feet, the guy you called to enforce the backdoor deals, the guy who fell in love with every girl in the room, was now trying to counsel people.

"I can't believe this guy is a chaplain now, can you believe it?" He went on and on, one seedy tale after another. The crowd was laughing at first, but soon they had the look. The look of worry and caution. They had heard about some kind of *past* before, but that day they got to see that all my sins were not the fun kind.

I wished the guy could believe that I was a different person than who I was before. But I replayed it all. Every terrible, humiliating moment in a nauseating loop. Then the guilt, the shame, the stomach-sick tendrils racing up my gut, the stench in my nostrils, my chest pulling in, like coughing in reverse. I heard that little voice: *You're the same guy, you haven't changed, I know who you really are.*

And as simple as it may seem, I thought of the verse:

> *If any man be in Christ,*
> *he is a new creature:*
> *old things are passed away;*
> *behold, all things are become new.*[28]

I remember reading that Paul was so excited when he wrote these words, they read a little funny. In the Greek, Paul wrote, *If anyone in Christ, new creation; the old has passed; behold! new has come.*

I think this truth was a big deal for Paul. You may know his story already: he had made a career of knocking off Christians. Then God knocked him off his high horse and he became a Christian. As far as the church knew, if he was made new in Christ, then he was a new guy to them, too. Paul was probably serving at churches with family members of people he had persecuted. I'm imagining his regret. His nightmares. His tears and apologies for these families, only for them to say, "You've been re-made, Paul. No more guilt. You're not who you were. You're new." I think about how much this tenderized him and galvanized him. I'm imagining how liberating and heart-rending this newness was for Paul.

That's grace, about as much grace as anybody can stand. It's the hope of an undeserved love. It's the thing we most need, but the hardest thing to give. Yet God, we're told, is willing to give it freely, at His own expense, wave after wave of it, like galaxies poured from His cup.

It doesn't mean we're not accountable. There must be reparations, justice, repentance. That sometimes means people will leave, and rightfully so; nobody had to stick around Paul or me, if they didn't want to. But *grace* means we're no longer imprisoned to compensating for the "old-me." I'm not bound to pay off my debt by a somber, head-hanging modesty. The old-me is dead. The old-you is gone. It takes no less than the piercing love of God to put it to death, to die. It takes no less than the restoring love of God to give us breath, to make us alive. In that sort of love, no one is ever the same person they were before. It means that I don't forget where I came from, but I can't forget where I'm going.

The shame lifted for me then. Not all the way, no. Maybe enough to breathe a little.

I pray you can have that sort of freedom. I pray for that for my future children, and yours, that they'll be more than the story of Adam.

YOU WILL FIND ALL YOU NEED

Dear future daughter,

Sooner or later, you're going to have questions.

You might ask about why you have certain tics and twitches. Why you seem to get angry as fast as you can throw a fist. Why you have those midnight loops and ruminations and endless repeats of harsh words in your head. You might realize you're more depressed or tired or anxious than everyone else. You might not cope as easily with stress or bad news or a bad test grade or a rejection letter or a boy's rejection. You might feel sick in your body and the doctor will tell you that all your tests came back fine—and you'll say you're not fine, because it feels like your guts are twisted around your lungs.

You will laugh like me, loudly and heehawing down the hallway. But you will cry like me too, sometimes uncontrollably, locked in a room for hours until you can't breathe.

I have always been afraid of seeing me in you. The echo. It's my brain, bleeding over into yours. It isn't fair. It isn't your fault. It isn't exactly mine, either. But I get it that you'll be mad at me. You'll see a part of me in the way you move. The way I move—the way you might move too—is like one of my legs is shorter than the other. Those missing inches were taken from me, a part of my soul clipped by the hardness of the world. You might be missing some of those inches too. I hope to God that you won't be. I can hope, can't I?

I'm sorry. I have always been sorry. I was always certain that something was so irreparably sick in me that I would pass it on to you. I have always been scared that one day you'll figure it out, and you'll bust down the door and shout, "Why? Why did you think it was okay to make me when you're not okay?"

It was all I could give you. I wish I had more. But I don't. I wish I could protect you. From myself, sure, and from the eventualities of life. But I can't. I wish so badly. But I can't. I don't know how I can love you enough.

Here's what I know. You are not a blank page—but you can write a different story too. And yes, you will take on my bad. But you will take on my good, too. I'd like to think you'll be all the good that I've ever wanted to be.

When I was a young boy, I found a bird outside my father's business.

The bird was dying. I placed him in a shoebox. I went outside to catch worms and beetles. I made a circle of insects around the bird, for food. I spoke to him. I sang to him. I prayed over him. Slowly, he died. I cried for a long time. I buried him where I found him and placed a white daisy over his grave. I replaced that daisy for many days. I was a boy. I was not strong enough. I found the strength. And the part of me that sang to the bird has never been taken away. No awful thing in life ever took that from me. No awful thing in life can ever take away your heart for the sparrow.

I was a young teen. My mother, your grandmother, came home stumbling. She made it to her room. She spoke and her breath stung my eyes. I turned her to her side. I tucked her in. I prayed over her. I never should've been in that situation. I was only a boy. I was not strong enough. I found the strength.

When I was older, my mother told me a story. It was about how she came here. She came to this country as a young woman. She hardly knew the language. She was a salesperson. She learned the language. She worked at a candy factory. All she could afford to eat was candy. Her teeth hurt every day. She sang nights at a jazz lounge to pay the bills. She became pregnant with me by a man she hardly knew. She carried the same illness that I carry and that maybe you will carry too. She would stare at a wall for hours. She drank. She ran away. She ran her own business. She raised me. She gave me the story she could not have herself. She was not strong enough. But she found the strength. She carried darkness, but she carried light too. She gave me both, and the light is shining brighter.

Your light will be so bright. I'm sure of it. But either way, I will love you so much it will make you sick.

I promise you, you will find the strength. You will find it because I did. You will find it, just as surely as God found me and led me to you.

CHAPTER 8

Navigating Family of Origin: Tracing an Echo

Family Dynamics

Once you're a parent,
you're the ghost of your children's future.
—COOPER, *INTERSTELLAR*[1]

I visited Ms. Ransom six times before lung cancer took her life. Ms. Ransom, first name Henrietta, or as she liked to be called, Rietta, had the largest family I had ever seen: two adopted children, eight brothers and sisters, her mother and stepfather, and about two dozen aunts, uncles, and cousins. She was a widow; her husband had died in a car accident a year after their only child Jaycie was born. Jaycie also died in the accident. Rietta raised her late husband's two children as her own.

I remember Rietta as sharp, funny, crackling, the kind of person you would want to speak at your wedding or funeral or before the big game. She was about my age. She had been a therapist, the first one in her entire family line to get a doctorate.

Of all my patients, Rietta was that *one,* the landmark, the star patient, the one who gave me more than I had ever given her. Her story was full of secrets, twists, and turns, a neon labyrinth of dark corners and stunning revelations. It might not have happened exactly the way that I'm going to tell it, but stories are like sculptures, an attempt to catch the details in the marble, and even for a brief flicker they can bring somebody back to life. In her story was part of mine—and maybe part of yours too.

1. CORKBOARD CONSPIRACY

On our first visit, Rietta wanted to tell me about this moral dilemma with her family.

Rietta wanted to die peacefully, no compressions or chemicals or shocks, but she knew her family hated the idea. Legally, the patient gets the say-so. But for a patient, it was never that simple.

"I know it's *my* decision," Rietta told me, her voice strong and clear, "thanks to our healthcare laws. I know the protocol, the doctors are all supposed to speak to me 'in private' to make sure I can speak for myself. But it isn't so easy when your family is everything." She said the last word in long syllables: *eh-vuh-ree-thing.* "These doctors here don't get it. You get it, don't you?"

I nodded. I got it, all right.

"Or I'm just being stubborn," she said, laughing. "When I was a

166

therapist I got to see what was wrong with everybody, and I could get them somewhere—but goodness, I can't do the same for me."

She told me she had all the education in the world about *family dynamics*,[2] but it could go out the window in a hurry. "That's how crazy that family can get you. I'm so *nice* when they're not around. I know how to be in my head, but my family comes around, my brains get wrapped up in knots and I can't see past my nose. I'm good at all the lofty shop talk, but in practice the whole business is brutal." Rietta looked me up and down and said, "I know y'all chaplains do a training program and pick your old scabs. It's good training—until it isn't. Your wife or your dad says that one thing, the roof comes off right quick."

We laughed about that. Rietta continued. "I can see all of this like a road map, or maybe a blueprint. All the stuff my parents passed on. *Multigenerational transmission.* The cycles of tics and behaviors and traditions. My role in the mess. Did you learn that in your classes?"

I said that I did.

"Have you done the genogram yet?"

I said that I had.

"Goodness, wasn't it alarming?"

"Very alarming," I said. I got nervous suddenly; I had come to the room for the patient and now the patient was doing a number on me.

Rietta noticed my pause. "You don't have to say more," she said. "My genogram was like one of those corkboards with the yarn that detectives use in the movies. Spaghetti on a corkboard, connecting everything."

I smiled at the thought. I loved that kind of stuff.

The genogram, by the way, is like a drawing of a family tree that goes back a few generations, but it highlights things such as addiction, abuse, affairs, mental illness, divorce, cut-offs, or over-involvement. You can color-code the genogram and it ends up looking like a Pollock nightmare. I recommend it. You'll see the inherited patterns and repeated loops pulsing off the page. The good news is that the more you know your family, the more you know yourself—and the more you can confront the unknown in your life, the less it will control you for the rest of your life.

I asked, "What did that mean for you, Ms. Ransom? The cork-board spaghetti, I mean."

"Ah, a very good counseling question." Rietta coughed into a napkin and it came away with a line of brown and green. She tugged at her nasal cannula and glanced away. "I expected all the patterns. Alcoholism, separation and divorce, all kinds of violence, the entanglements. I went back four generations and there were twelve cases of sexual assault. Twelve. You know how many didn't get reported? Twelve."

Rietta took a long breath, as long as she could, and let it out fast. I saw something in her face, but it passed quickly. "I think what did surprise me," she said, "was how awful it felt to break the pattern."

"It felt awful?"

"It feels awful still. On two levels: I felt awful because some of my family was so resistant. They didn't like the idea of me trying to better myself. Maybe they were threatened, or they felt bad they couldn't do it themselves. It's hard to see the next in line do better than the first in line. But I also felt awful because *I didn't want to break the pattern.* I was so comfortable with the family story, to change it felt like I was betraying some deep part of me. You learned about that in family systems, right? *Homeostasis.* Every system is fighting to get back to its room temperature, to its own status quo. An alcoholic tries to quit, his family gets mad because they can't save him anymore."

She looked far off somewhere. I got that look too. I got that look a lot.

"I don't want to feel bad about it," Rietta said, "but I do. In my bones, I feel it. It's almost like I need to carry on my family dysfunction just to get right. My goodness, chaplain. I'm doomed to repeat all my history, and I'm doomed when I don't."

I thought about what Rietta said, that family has a way of reminding you about your place, but just as likely, you almost *want* to stay in place. Those dynamics have a way of getting established early and aggressively: some of us become co-parents or caretakers or victims or runaways, some of us become the perpetual Older Sibling or Prodigal Son or Favorite Kid, and even if we escape our family situations, we still slip back into the former way of things. Part of that is because our families won't let us forget, and part of that is because we always want to remember.

To some degree, we're all finding a surrogate family with substitute parts, a bunch of scrap metal nomads, sliding into old grooves. Trying to *get right.*

"I think," Rietta said, lifting her hands as they shook, spreading them as far as she could, "that I'm on the verge of some big discovery. A big bow tie to wrap this all up. A solution to the corkboard. Or I'm just a crazy lady on fentanyl with stage four lung cancer. Am I talking crazy?"

No, I told her. You are not talking crazy.

— — —

I was getting to another patient when my wife texted me: *Your dad is in the hospital. It's serious.* She found out from my step-mother, so it wasn't anything my dad wanted me to know.

He was about an hour away. Thirty minutes later, I got to his bedside. He looked pretty bad. I had seen a lot by now in the hospital, but I could have ranked my dad in the lower percentile. His face was a bold yellow color and his eyes were an inch deep. His stomach had become a basketball overnight and he reported a solid ten on the pain scale. The doctor said he needed surgery, but like I expected, my dad said, "No." It was the kind of surgery he needed to live. Sure, he wanted to live, but in his words, "I haven't been to the hospital in forty years, I'll be fine." The recovery was too long, he said. He wanted to go back to work. He had important plans. Very important.

My dad, by the way, is a scary guy. Like I said before, he was a second lieutenant in the Vietnam War. He was a POW and escaped with his bare hands. He's a ninth degree black belt, which is the highest you can get, and though he is nearing eighty years old, he still teaches at his dojo.

I mean, my dad can break a guy in half, but I think the most impressive thing I have ever seen him do is chop an apple into four perfectly even slices with the edge of his hand. Swoop, swoop, right through the core, and I got to share with three of my friends. I was seven at the time. It was really something.

I wanted to tell my dad to do the surgery, but I had never asked my dad to do anything before. That was the arrangement. I would tell my friends about it and they would blink. The young defer to the elderly and have to comply with their wishes. That was that. All the bowing and eyes to the floor was really serious stuff.

All I could reply was, "Yes, sir." Not *Yeah,* or *Okay,* or *Sure pops,* but *Yessir.*

A part of me had to speak up though. It was ridiculous, to let him turn down surgery. It was more ridiculous that I couldn't say anything.

2. ELECTRIFIED CURRENT

"Chaplain," Rietta told me, "I need you to see this."

For our second visit, we had scheduled a family meeting. What that meant was, the palliative care team would step in—physician, social worker, nurse, and chaplain—and the patient and her family would be informed of what was happening.

Rietta had asked me to come a few minutes early. She told me she wanted to change from a Full Code to DNR, Do Not Resuscitate. She leaned in and said, "If I code, I want to go. But I want my family to be on board. I won't decide this without them. It sounds silly, maybe, but I would rather go through the horror of resuscitation than the heartache of choosing against family."

I asked, "How can I be of help for you?"

Rietta wanted me to referee, to manage the tension. "You'll see us go at it, all of us a bunch of live wires in the room," she said, "and you'll see the current. I need you to advocate for me. It'll be like rerouting a river from north to south. I know it's a big request. They don't trust doctors and family won't hear it from family. They got to hear it from someone else. For you, *a man of God,* they'll get out the fine china."

Rietta's family was there, about three dozen of them in the room. Rietta's mother, Norma, was towering over her daughter, practically vibrating at the joints. Rietta's stepdad, Henry, was near the edge of the bed, a large man hiding in a cap and thick glasses, unmoving. Behind his dark wet eyes, I could see a mile of worry. Rietta had told me that her mother Norma was an *overfunctioner:* "She gets into take-charge mode and fixes everything without feeling anything." Rietta's stepdad was an *underfunctioner:* "He shuts down because he feels too much and gets overwhelmed."[3] All around Norma and Henry were siblings and cousins and aunts and uncles, elbow to chin with hardly a space between them.

The palliative team managed to squeeze around the bed. Usually, the physician would give updates and be the first to leave; the chaplain would pick up the fallout and be the last to leave.

As soon as the palliative team left, Rietta's mother Norma got into it. Like Rietta had asked me, I watched.

"Henrietta," Norma said, "you need to think about us too, baby."

"Momma, I'm doing that. I'm doing just that."

"You need to fight, baby. Can't you do that?"

"That's *all* I've been doing, Momma. That's all I'm doing. I'm running out of fight."

"Rietta, you want to just give up? You're going to give up on all of us?"

"Momma, do you hear what the doctors are saying?"

"I don't trust these people, they don't know the doctor of all doctors, they haven't seen what the Lord can do."

"Momma, I believe that too, but I don't want to—"

Then a lot of people started talking at once. Groups of twos and threes turned at each other. Alliances formed. I could see triangles, the two sides of the room discussing Rietta's wishes, both for and against.

For a second there I was taken out of the scene, like I had gotten a glimpse of the boom mic and the stagehands and the catwalk. I could see the expansion and collapse in peoples' shoulders, the way that everybody snapped or sighed, leaned close or fell back. I could see the electrified current running back and forth, invisible wires in conflict and connection, separate human wills colliding. The struggle for power.

What I haven't been able to get out of my head to this day was a little boy about ten years old sitting near me with his younger brother. Each time the room got loud, the older boy would cover his brother's ears. That older brother was about as alert a kid as I've ever seen, eyes darting around and taking in every word. I had a feeling that both of them had been set on a path that day, a path as narrow as the distance between their ears.

And I could see that Rietta was a different person with her family. I mean, we all are—family makes you that crazy, she had said—but the change was still something. With me, Rietta had seemed self-assured; she had said knowledgeable things with a deep satisfaction, her eyes locked and animated. But with her family she was two feet tall; she at turns yelled and cried and pointed fingers, and when she got swatted down, she stayed down. By the end she had pulled the covers up to her chin.

I tried to referee the room like Rietta had asked, but I got rolled over just as fast as she did. By the time the meeting was over, I was sweating through my socks, and I felt like we were in worse shape than before. I had that funny sort of hangover you get after you give a public speech and the only response is a guy clearing his throat.

Rietta asked me if I could come back the next day. She smiled at me, but it was a thin smile, the kind you have to wear to keep yourself from busting at the seams.

3. BUSTED CONTRACTS

"I'm sorry, chaplain."

Rietta was sitting in a chair on our third meeting. A shaft of light from the window just missed her, nearing her toes. She was under a blanket, one of hers, a quilt sort of deal with—no kidding—pictures of her family's faces on all the patches.

"No, no," I said. "I'm sorry myself."

"Goodness," she said. "I got lost. I couldn't see straight. It was embarrassing."

Rietta asked me if the chaplains had learned about *self-differentiation*.[4] I said that we had. A person with high self-differentiation is said to have a strong sense of their own identity; a person with low self-differentiation is *fused* or *enmeshed*, all mixed up with others, bound by groupthink, a bundle of re-flexes to everyone around them, including themselves.

"You could see I was all fused up," Rietta said, smiling only a little. She explained it like this: "I see myself on a road trip, my family smushed together in a car, all talking at once. They're over my shoulder, under my neck, in my face. They all tell me turn here, exit there, stop here, don't stop. And I do whatever they ask. I want them to be all right, that's why. I have these *loyalty contracts*, unspoken promises and conditions. I do things for my family that would look miserable to somebody looking through the window. Don't we do that for family though? Someone says, 'You're being used,' and I say, 'It's sacrifice.' Even if it hurts me, I'm obligated. They got me early before I had time to read the small print. And that bleeds over to all my interactions. I had so much practice giving myself away, I'm a discount dollar store. I end up secretly hating everyone. Or confused. Or exhausted."

I knew what she was saying. My Korean tradition had an active type of loyalty called *hyodo,* or filial piety. It was our sworn duty to serve our parents and ancestors, both with provision and in memory. It might sound goofy, but for us it was serious business.

Rietta added quickly, "The contracts are not all bad. I don't want to say my mom is wrong or evil. She has a good reason to be the way she is. Did I tell you, my birth dad died of cancer? Same as mine, the lungs. My mom made our home a hospice. Fed my dad, changed him, bathed him. A whole year, she took care of him. She was already Type A before, but this made her Type A+. Now it's like she's losing my dad all over again. So I feel like I owe her to stay alive. My final contract, you know? I know this gives her meaning.

My dad did the chemo, he kept on trying to live so that my mom could keep living. Part of me thinks she married Henry, my stepdad, because he's so helpless. My mom likes it that way."

We sat in this for a while. I knew that a gulf had closed, the invisible wall between both of us dissipating.

I asked Rietta, "Is there a way to break out of all this but still respect your family?" I was asking mostly for her sake, but some for mine, too.

Rietta looked away for a moment, through the window, to a world she was never going back to.

"Maybe I'm looking at it all wrong," Rietta said. "There's got to be a way I can be for me *and* for them. I don't want to cave in, but I don't want to cut off. You know, not dependence or independence. *Interdependence.* That golden middle. Some of my clients made it. They had families that were like a choir but you could hear the individual voices."

Rietta told me that self-differentiated people could boldly announce themselves without getting pushy about it. They could make thoughtful choices outside the groupthink but still within the group. They could be both supportive and critical about what others were demanding. They could play by the family's rules without getting played by them.[5] Theoretically, anyway.

I wish I could tell you it's easy to become a person like this, just by describing the person you ought to be. But it takes work. Real work. It takes a million conversations with your parents or siblings or children before they begin to see you as a real person, with a life all your own. It takes a thousand persistent reminders and sit-downs before your family gets *their* version of you out of their heads and sees *you*, the growing, maturing, complex person that you are and want to be. It could take your whole life to show *you are your own household*, even if that house is simply your body and your brain. But it starts with the conversation, with your voice rising—not above theirs, but through, and with, in the key of the golden middle. And the reverse is true too, I think. You find depth in your family, and the reasons *why*, and the backstory, and your family comes alive. You might find, even, that your family is made of neither gold, nor glass. They're made of guts, just like you. They need grace, like you do. When a person becomes alive to you, you get to see where they're hurting and what they need to mend.

"Am I being too poetic?" Rietta asked.

No, I told her. I liked the poetry. I liked it just fine.

Rietta took a long breath, then laughed to herself. "Goodness, yesterday was crazy, wasn't it? But that's how dialogue goes. I'd say that crazy is progress."

4. A VAULTED HISTORY

I was working an overnight a few days later and it was nearly three in the morning when I got a page. I recognized the room number. Rietta needed to talk.

When I got there, she was in the chair again, this time the moonlight thrown across her face. Rietta had been crying, or yelling, or both. She had more pronounced lines in her cheeks than just a few days ago. The cancer had taken some more. Always taking, pulling, stealing: time, laughter, movement, dignity, all of it devoured by a fistful of voracious malignant cells with no mind of their own. It was a ruthless slippery tunnel into the ground, lit by radiation and shriveled bags of chemo, a forced march into nowhere.

I sat down without a noise. There was silence for a while. Rietta did not look at me. Her eyes were outside again. She held a pen in her hand almost like a cigarette, and for a second the room looked as smoky as a jazz lounge.

"Chaplain," Rietta said, "they never told me that death makes you think such funny things." Her words rolled out with almost drunken purpose. She tried to laugh, but it didn't happen. Couldn't happen, for all I knew.

She continued. "The less time I have, the more the *fog* clears. The pain does something to clear away the smear. Everything's so silly to me now. These men on television; they call themselves experts. It's all a bowl of cotton candy and spider webs. Do I sound cynical? I promise I'm not. I think I'm sober." Then she did laugh. "Of course, mostly I'm just in pain and that's all I can think of."

Rietta pointed the pen at me without looking and said, "Tell me, what kinds of things require you to make a mandatory report?"

"If you're currently abusing someone," I said, "or if you have plans to. Otherwise, I'm a vault."

"My husband Roy," she said, her voice unshaking, "the one who died. The car accident. I'm sorry to say that I killed him."

We were quiet for a while again. Then Rietta looked at me, and it was a look that could have knocked me over.

"My husband—*late* husband—was molesting both his girls. I couldn't let it happen to my baby. Not to my daughter Jaycie. Can you see my anger? Chaplain, all his family knew. They knew. They just let it happen. I prayed every day this man, this monster, would die. I prayed with hate through my teeth. I only told my stepfather, Henry, about what was happening. A few weeks later, Roy's car slipped off a bridge. For a second I was free. And then they told me that my baby Jaycie was in the car, too."

Rietta took a breath, and then she let out the longest cough I had ever heard from anyone in my life. She was doubled over, almost a full circle, making the noise of a runaway chainsaw, and I nearly went to grab the nurse. Rietta waved a hand. She continued like it never happened.

"I don't know if my prayer killed Roy," she said, "or if my stepfather messed with the car—" She stopped herself from finishing the thought. "I had told you there were twelve cases of sexual abuse in my family. Including his daughters, that's fourteen. And Jaycie—we know, but we don't. We look loud in this room, don't we, chaplain? Arguing like we do. About fixing me. It's easier. We're quiet about the things that really hurt."

I thought about the little boy in the room, Rietta's nephew, covering the ears of his younger brother.

"Some people," Rietta said, jaw clenching, "by blood are in your family, but they're not *with* your family. They're not *for* you. I believe everyone can be redeemed. But I don't believe everyone is supposed to wait for that to happen. You want to assume that everybody has the same good will that you do, but they don't. The worst part is when nobody believes that the monster lives in your house. The worst part is when they use the 'family card' so they don't have to look under the bed."

I shuddered. I wanted to weep. I felt the weight of this dark, terrible secret that Rietta had held for so long, the evil done against those two young girls, the cost of trying to make it right, the impossible choices that were made.

I thought of what Rietta had said: *Some people by blood are in your family, but they're not* with *your family.* And she was right. Sometimes you do need to walk away from your next of kin, if that's what it comes to. Attachment by blood is a happenstance, not a contract. If anything, blood ought to be more reason for kindness, not permission for cruelty. All this family talk might make you think that you need to stick by them, and forgiveness is important, sure. I know the healing power of letting go of the wound. But forgiveness isn't letting the evil back in your life; it isn't enabling or pampering or coddling; it isn't giving away the spare key to abuse. You might have a lot of people telling you, "They'll always be your family," and that remains true. It's as true as a hurricane is made of air—air that happens to flatten an entire city and air that you don't need to invite to Thanksgiving dinner.

Rietta blinked away tears. "This doesn't excuse what I did. I killed them. And justice has to be done right. I don't want to be resuscitated because that's fair. I deserve what's happening to me. Have you ever heard of such a thing?"

No, I said, wiping my face. I said I had not.

Rietta flicked her pen, as if flicking ashes, letting them swirl into the purple of the dark.

"Chaplain," she said, looking at the floor, "I feel I'm dying very soon. I don't want to take this with me. When you tell people my story, don't leave this part out. Don't clean it up. I tried so hard to clean up the ugly side of things—but they don't get clean that way. They only get quiet. And I've been quiet for so long. The voices we carry, they're so hard and heavy. They're the elephant in the room, but the elephant grows out of control, filling up the doors and halls and windows and they choke us out, like this cancer eating away at me. Is that too on the nose?"

No, I told her. It was on the nose enough.

"I heard confession is good for the soul," she said, and laughed. A single, raspy laugh. "Chaplain, that's it. It's time to have it out. I need to get this all in the open."

5. ALL IN THE OPEN

Rietta asked for me the next morning.

When I got there, Rietta's mother Norma and stepfather Henry were at bedside. Norma was standing over her daughter; Henry sitting but tightened. For a moment they made a tableau, a chiaroscuro of lit faces caught in the middle of their personalities.

"Good morning," Norma said, shaking my hand very hard. "I guess you didn't get enough of us, chaplain." She looked around, and without warning she laughed exactly three times.

Henry nodded at me. He was no longer wearing glasses or a cap. His face looked tougher than I remembered, and in his eyes was a kind of flame behind glass. It seemed to grow large and clear.

I took my place across from Norma, and immediately Rietta began.

"Momma," she said, reaching for her mother's hand, "I want to go with the DNR. What are you so scared about?"

"Baby," Norma said, pulling back her hand, "do *not* use that psychology on me. You're always putting everybody square. Now you're educated, you trying to educate everyone else."

"Momma, we are *not* doing that today. Don't be mad you were never educated."

That one stung. Norma flinched. "You say things like that in front of the chaplain? You bring him here like he's supposed to—"

"I brought him for *me*, not to make you feel any kind of way, I—"

"Well it don't feel that way, you're just—"

It went on like this for a while, and then Henry stood up. Both his hands were shaking. He grabbed one of his wife's hands, and one of Rietta's, and nobody talked for a minute.

Then Henry, quietly enough, said "I'm scared. I'll tell you why. I'm scared about how it'll be. I don't know the words, Rietta, like you do. But the way I see it, you and me and your mom, we've been using each other."

Norma gasped. Henry kept going.

"I mean in a good way now. I mean the way that makes sense to us. Your mom wants to take care of you to make up for your father. You're wanting to make up for Jaycie. And I get something out of letting your mom pamper me real nice. Do you see where I'm going with this?"

Rietta nodded. Norma seemed to lose all the pep in her bones.

"Rietta, if you don't fight," Henry said, his voice hardly a whisper, "your mom will think she failed you. If you do fight, you'll think you failed Jaycie. I don't know, Rietta. I just want you to decide for you, not because you're feeling guilty or anything else."

Norma lifted her daughter's hand to her own face. And like that, Norma wept really hard, about as loud as I had ever heard.

She had looked really tough before with her family in the room, hands on hips as she asked the doctors a hundred questions, skeptical of every answer, talking over her daughter, but I could *see* her now, a woman who had been strong for too long. I could see that nobody had let her be weak—including herself. I felt sad for her then. Not pity. I mean, real heartbreak. I saw her sheer loneliness, the hardness of losing her husband, her granddaughter, and now her daughter, all the pieces of herself. She probably thought she looked weak in this second, letting her guard down, but to me, she was stronger than I had ever seen her.

"Rietta, what am I without you?"

"Momma," Rietta said, almost sitting up, "everything good in me is *you*. You know that."

Norma finally sat in a chair. "You're like your father," she said. "So smart. So set."

Rietta and Norma were just about eye to eye, and they really did look alike. Both leaning forward, eyes sharp and lucid: they could have been twins in silhouette.

Norma looked at me and caught me staring. She said, "You want to stand there or you want to grab us some tissues?"

They all laughed. I reached in my pocket and produced a box of new tissues, and they laughed again.

6. WHAT IT ALL MEANS

I was paged early in the morning for a pre-surgery visit. Rietta had made a compromise with her family: she was going to get the DNR, but undergo surgery to remove part of a lobe. The hope was to extend Rietta's life a bit, maybe by a few months. The surgery was just as likely to kill her. Rietta knew the risks, that anything could go wrong.

"Chaplain," she said, beaming. She was wearing a surgical cap, a fresh gown, knees tucked up to her shoulders. "We have to quit meeting this way."

It was my turn to laugh. "How do you feel?" I asked.

"I feel like I ought to know better."

"Ms. Ransom," I said, "would you like me to pray with you before surgery?"

"Yes," she said, "but goodness, this 'Ms. Ransom' stuff has to go." She tried to smile, but she leaned over in a fit of coughs.

I drew close to her bedside, and Rietta clasped my hand in both of hers.

"Chaplain, remember the thing I said the other day? About being on the verge of discovering something really big?"

Yes, I told her. I remembered. I was curious if she was ever going to come back to it.

"A few nights ago," Rietta said, eyes misty, "I was sitting in that chair by the window, my very favorite chair the last few weeks, and there was a strange little bird outside. I had never seen such a bird. She was a beautiful brown bird with a blue streak across her face, two curling antennas like hair flowing down her sides, a long tail fanning out with a luscious green tint at the edges. I wondered what had brought her here. Why was this beautiful bird at the window of the sixth floor of a hospital? Was it random? A mistake? Instinct? Chance?

"I thought about what makes a bird feel like she's home. It hit me, chaplain, what it all means. I was thinking about the way we repeat our history, or how we fight that history, and it's like we're always looking for the home we used to have, or we want the one we never got to have. And it's always back there somewhere, in another time when everything we went through was for the first time. There's nothing else like that feeling. When life was pure and new, when the pages were crisp.

"There's no going back, but there's no running away, either. We try to find a new foundation. But it has to be built with the life we already know. Like when we hang up our pictures in a new place. Am I talking crazy?"

No, I told her. You are not talking crazy.

"The morning after I saw that bird," Rietta said, "I got my appetite back a little bit and I ordered a grapefruit. I hadn't eaten one of those in so long, chaplain. I smelled that grapefruit and I was transported. My father used to slice a grapefruit in half and sprinkle some sugar on the halves and we got two spoons and we'd dig out the chunks. I would look at my father over my spoon and he would look at me and wink, and I felt safe. It was like looking into the face of God, all this goodness in a grapefruit. We look for *that*, always looking. Or it looks for us."

Rietta took a deep breath and leaned forward in the way she did, full of intent. "It seemed like all my classes taught that we're supposed to run from family patterns. Sometimes we have to. But all of that's still *home* for me. There is value in where I came from. I don't need to therapy all of it away. All this we learn about becoming a self: is that really the goal? My family *is* me, after all. I am my family. What my family wants is also what *I* want. My voice is theirs, too. Wherever I fly, I fly with them. I can't do it alone. My goodness, I wouldn't ever want to."

Rietta closed her eyes. "This minister told me one time," she said, almost smiling, "that we are orphans and exiles, looking to belong again in the arms of God. The minister said that this has always been the story of God, to be our father. If so, I think that is beautiful. I want to believe that."

Rietta coughed, but just once. "I'm ready now," she said. "I'm ready to see God. I'm ready to see Jaycie."

That's how I remember Rietta now. Leaned forward, eyes closed, in prayer, her small frail hand covering mine, her spirit as tall as the room we were in. I don't remember my prayer. I remember her face though, like I was looking into the face of God, and in it, a place to finally belong.

A WORD FOR YOU:

Orphan Birds Under Construction

I've thought a lot about Rietta's last words to me. How we are orphan birds. How we build our home from the old and the new. How a hint of grapefruit can contain all the goodness in the world.

I have thought a lot about the things from my family that were gifts to me, and other things that I had to rebuild. I have thought about my history as a road map, a map that kept me stuck in circles, sometimes at a pit stop, many times just a pit. I've wanted to throw out that map, to get rid of the sheer embarrassment of growing up in such a strange and unstable family—but after all, they were *my* family, and they were the only home I knew, and to tell you the truth, I wouldn't take all of it back. A lot of it was good even, and had taken me soaring.

I think if you can make sense of your map, of your history, of the heirlooms and legends and loyalty contracts and severed ties, you get a bird's-eye view of what works—and what doesn't. You see the potholes and pitfalls. You find you're not inextricably linked to dead ends and dysfunction. You can start the painful work of digging up new roads. You find you do have the power to break old patterns, mostly because you've been down that alley enough.

You also find value in some of the old roads. It isn't your entire value, but you find the rituals and traditions that are as warm as a fireplace. You find the smell of sea breeze and woodwork and stadiums and fish bait and freshly steamed rice. You pass down the stories of courage. Of huddling on holidays. How your father barely made rent. How your mother had to cut your hair because the barbershop was a luxury. How some evenings, dinner wasn't tense, but filled by a flow of laughter. And you find value even in stories of cowardice, because they are universal and human, and having all your ugliness out in the open is the start of choosing something else.

ARC PLOT DENOUEMENT: MY SON, DON'T FORGET

I was holding my father's hand.

My dad, like I was saying, needed the surgery, but I knew he was too proud about it, and I had to move past my fear and say something without saying too much.

I knew the thing I really wanted to say.

What, are you crazy? You have to do this surgery or you'll die.

187

But he would never go for that. So I found the thing between worlds. The golden middle, the thing he could hear.

"Please do the surgery. For me."

That was the thing. My dad still operated out of family honor. All those traditions. That was the language he spoke. It was mine, too. And maybe that was a mean trick, to bind him to his own code. But I wondered if it was really a trick. I'd like to think I was meeting him where he was.

He said yes. He would do the surgery if it was for me. What a weird thing, that was.

I came to see him the moment he was rolled out of the OR. He was groggy. The drugs. The first thing he told me was, "My body is not my body." He giggled. I found out we have the same giggle.

We got back to his room and he asked, "How did it go?"

"Your surgery?"

"Your speech," he said.

I had told my dad earlier in the week that I was speaking at a seminar. I was surprised he remembered.

"It went well," I said. "It all went really well."

My dad giggled again. Then he reached out, put a hand on my shoulder, and said, "I'm proud of you, son. Don't forget. I have always been proud of you. Thank you for—"

And he fell asleep. I suppose it was the drugs talking. I suppose I was okay with that.

I whispered, *Yes, sir.*

I watched him dream. I stayed for a while. I watched my father, full of dreams.

7. YOU SAW ME

"Chaplain?" The surgeon met me in the hallway. "I'm sorry."

"No," I said. "No," I said again.

Rietta's time of death was 11:17.

"Can you go with me to tell her family?" the surgeon asked. "Is that okay, chaplain?" He was barely composed. "My mom—well, she's been gone only a little while."

"Yes," I said. "You have a hard job," I added.

"My good friend," he said, "so do you."

Everyone was there: about fifty people in the third floor waiting room outside the OR. I paused at the doorway before they noticed me. A few were praying. A few were laughing. They were all huddled close.

One more second, I thought, *to see them this way.*

Their grief was loud. Norma hardly moved, but Henry fell to his side and wailed. Norma stroked his head, telling him it was okay, it was okay.

I stayed with them for three hours. I said very few words. Mostly I sat with Norma and Henry. Mostly I said, "I'm sorry."

Family shuffled in and out, and by the third hour the stream of people settled. Henry asked if I could step into the hallway for a moment. He had Rietta's quilt, the one with all the family's faces. It was draped around his shoulders, like a cape.

We went to the hallway and Henry placed a hand on my shoulder. I thought of my father's hand and the way that fathers can be; tall and comforting, immutable but grounded. He squeezed, but only a little.

"Chaplain," Henry said. "You need to know . . . the things I said yesterday, about Norma and Rietta using each other, you need to know that wasn't me."

"Wasn't you?"

"It was Rietta. She asked me to say those things. She said when things got to be too heated, that I needed to say something. I didn't know what. So Rietta gave me the words. The right words. She . . . she always knew what to say. My Henrietta was like nobody else."

I found myself fighting back tears. I told Henry, "She really was someone special."

"She was," Henry said, hiding those fierce eyes. "She is."

A few days later, I got a letter mailed to me at the office. It was from one Henrietta Rosita Ransom. In the envelope was a single sheet of hospital stationery.

This is what she wrote:

For a season, our stories met.

You saw me and stayed.

You are my family now.

Thank you, dear, for walking me home.

CHAPTER 9

Navigating Grief and Loss: Dreamboat River

The Impossible Goodbye

We kept the dead alive with stories.
— TIM O'BRIEN, *THE THINGS THEY CARRIED*[1]

I WON'T SOON FORGET

I was seeing hundreds of dead and dying people, and in my dreams, I'd see them.

In the hospital, I was a grief-catcher. I caught stories. I made space so people could weep and vent and throw things. I caught bodies. I caught memories. I caught the dead.

After a while, I began to hear them. I heard the dead in my sleep. I heard them in long hallways. I heard them at two in the morning.

I heard them in my car. I would turn and turn and turn—but sure, nobody was there.

In my dreams, their beds were sitting upright, and they weren't exactly dead, but they didn't move. They would stare. Glass, stone, eyes fixed. Their beds moved closer and closer until they were close enough to breathe my hair apart. I would wake up with my hands over my face, and I would reach over to my wife to see if she was still alive.

I'd wake up with the names of diseases in my mouth. *Arteriovenous malformation. Chronic Obstructive Pulmonary Disease. Congestive Heart Failure. Lupus. Crohn's. Non-Hodgkin's Lymphoma. Pancreatic cancer. Stage three. Stage four. End-stage.*

How I hated cancer. How I hate, hate, hated it.

I'd hear the pager. All the beeping. Sirens. I'd recite random things. *Vaso. Neo. Epi. Bicarb. Pulse check. ECMO. VAD. Dialysis. TPA for stroke. Auto-immune. Braden Scale. Glasgow Scale. Last seen normal at 2300. GSW. MVC. Stab wound. Self-inflicted. Thirty percent burns. Fall from twenty feet. Found face down. No pulse at the scene. Left-side droop. Altercation. Non-responsive. Combative. Ejected from vehicle. Alert and oriented times two. Found alone at the gas station. Time of death is ____.*

I would be driving home after a shift and see four kids laughing in a car, and I'd picture their car rolling over, the four of them rushed to the ER, unrecognizable. I would pick up the phone, making that call again: *This is the chaplain and I'm sorry to tell you but—*

Over and over again, I sat with crying spouses, crying fathers and mothers, last words, last goodbyes, the heart rate dwindling down to single digits, machines powered down, unplugged, swept room, new bed: start over again.

Of all things, I'd dream of paperwork. Mountains of it, just the horizon filled with stacks of ink-stained paper. Release of Body forms and grief packets and booklets and cards and flyers for funeral homes. Fill in the blank, confirm this name, who's the next of kin, sign on the last line. *Demographics,* they call it. It's the great equalizer. Everyone ends up a scribble on one of these pieces of paper, jammed in a folder with your entire life.

I dreamt of my patients.

I dreamt of them healthy and alive.

I dreamt they were okay.

I mean, wouldn't you?

THE WORST THING ABOUT GRIEF
IS WORSE THAN YOU THINK

I used to think that grief was about looking backward,
old men saddled with regrets
or young ones pondering should-haves.
I see now that it is about eyes squinting through tears
into an unbearable future.

—KATE BOWLER,

EVERYTHING HAPPENS FOR A REASON:
AND OTHER LIES I'VE LOVED[2]

I had thought the worst thing about grief was regretting the past. You know, all the roads not taken, the bad ones that were. But the worst thing is often the sudden sinkhole around the future. The roads that *can't* be taken. You peer into an imperceptible timeline where the edges of possibility have been eroded as fast as a thunderclap.

At the center of loss is the voice of a dream, the voice of a parallel life. The hardest stuff that happens, I have seen, is the stuff that doesn't.

My friend and fellow chaplain Rebecca told me that when her friend died, she felt two distinct pains: the *loss of secret connections*, all those inside jokes and shared language, and *lost promise*, the hope of more adventure.

They call that *intrapsychic grief*, the pain of losing what could've been and will never be. The loss around loss. The interruption of future. The theft of invested time. Hopes and plans and dreams that crashed mid-flight: a ghost of a ghost.

They tell you to turn the page. Accept it. Move on. Let go.

But I learned something different about grief from my patients and their families. I learned that getting through grief wasn't about *letting go* at all.

— — —

I see Irene. Irene tells me that grief feels like you're going crazy. I mean really insane.

"I see him," she says. We're sitting next to Irene's husband, who has been on life support for weeks. She knows he's gone already, but she can't make the decision yet. *That* decision. "I see him everywhere. At the corner of Waters and Linebaugh, he said something funny that made me laugh from one end of the street to the next. At the grocery store, we'd split apart so he'd get the meats and I'd get the veggies, and sometimes he'd meet me at the check-out with roses from the florist. I wait for him at the check-out. I forget he's not coming. I forget he's gone. But he isn't. I still see him. I *like* seeing him. Have I gone mad?"

When someone goes, their voice doesn't.

They're gone, but they're more here than ever.

"My world has stopped," Irene tells me, "and I want everybody to stop with me. But the world keeps going. Everyone tells me to get over it. Let him go. Could you do it, chaplain? Could you let a person go like that?"

Irene suddenly shouts at the ceiling. It startles me. Her scream is piercing. It's agony. She slaps her husband's arm. Hard.

"Is it always going to be like this?" She barely gets the words out. "How can you miss a person so much? How does anybody live the rest of their life this way? Really, have I gone mad?"

I've been trained to ask her all the chaplain questions: *Why do you think you've gone mad? What does "mad" mean to you? What does going mad feel like? Are you mad at me right now?*

But I tell her, "You're perfectly sane. You're the sanest person I've ever met."

"I bet you tell that to all your patients." Irene sort of laughs. "Tell me, does this get easier for anybody?"

"Not always. I heard there are good days and bad days. Grief is supposed to hit you in waves. The other thing I've heard is that the memories get warmer. Eventually the memory of those who are gone becomes a warm blanket that you can wear sometimes. Or, I guess, you learn to ride the waves. I'm mixing metaphors, but that's what I heard."

"Well, whoever said that was trying to be cute." Irene huffed. "I like it, I guess."

LETTING GO OF LETTING GO

Grief, I've learned, is a form of time travel, or maybe a time transplant. It's a way of reclaiming ruptured dreams. To see the dead again. To hear them again. Part of my job is to give grief a voice.

It probably seems uncouth to raise the dead that way. But when I've asked about the deceased, the family and friends usually unload. It's like they couldn't wait to. They have story after story of the dead, enough that I can see the barest outlines of the life that was lived, like David appearing out of the marble. You'd hear about the motorcycle he built from scratch or the other two heart attacks he survived or the gymnastics medal she won in fourth grade or how she had taken in fourteen rescue dogs after she had said two was too many. Even if the family hated the deceased, the family had a lot to say, maybe even more than if they loved him.

When given a chance, the grief was embraced.

That was not what I had expected. The way I've seen it, grief is depicted as a sort of logical progression from sadness to acceptance. It's always the end of a sad movie when the sad person quits visiting the graveyard and joins a spin class and finds a new lover and takes a shower. Our hospital's grief pamphlet has a picture of entering a deep valley with storm clouds overhead, only to emerge on a mountaintop with flowers at the summit.

See, I might tell a patient, *your grief will give way to this mountain here with flowers on top.*

Oh, thanks, a patient might say. *I'll remember that drawing the next time my body is wracked with horrific inconsolable agony over the death of my four-year-old.*

I've never liked that pamphlet. Or those movies. Or the idea that you'll be fine after a Hollywood montage. It's too clean. It makes me think of words like algorithm or trajectory or pro-jected outcomes. Chemicals and computers work that way. Not people, I don't think. Not you and not me.

I came to let go of the "letting go" idea. To me, that sort of grief process is the most compartmentalized ritual ever schemed. It rules that everything—the body, keepsakes, clothes, albums, treasures, and trinkets—goes into boxes and is thrust as far away as possible. Everything touched by death is severed, jettisoned, or pulverized. Death is considered a curse, a taboo topic of hushed tones and sour smells.

I've seen the end result of all that suppression. I've seen men and women beat their own chests, trying to shove down the memory of the dead. It was what they were taught to do. Con-fronting grief sounds like a crazy thing to do, after all. The irony, though, is that when you bury somebody too fast, you end up denying what they meant to you. Then their voice comes back in all kinds of ways, none of them good. And you end up disappear-ing a part of yourself too.

When grief is buried, it doesn't go away. It waits. It shouts. It demands to be heard.

Grief is a story gasping to be told.

THE PROCESS HAS A PROCESS

I think one of the most troublesome things I had to deal with at the hospital was handling somebody's attempts to shut down someone else's loss. In other words, a patient might be grieving, but a family member would come along and say, "Don't cry" and "It's all right" and "God's got it," and all those other unhelpful, hasty platitudes.

I'm in this room where a father keeps telling his daughter, "It's all in God's hands now, it's all God's will." The girl has lost both her feet in a car accident and her eyes are blank; she's looking past her dad, somewhere else, into another universe where the other driver had one less shot at the bar.

I want to tell her father, *Can't you be more sensitive? Don't you know it's a process? Can't you see that sort of cliché crap doesn't work?*

It's easy to see this dad as the bad guy. And sometimes, the guy who brushes off your pain really is the bad guy. But I started to think: *What other way would he have known?* All we ever hear about grief is how to tie it up with a bow made of steel and throw it in the ocean with the rest of the world's refuse. That's all he had been trained to do.

Besides, *maybe this was his initial way of processing.* This was his way of managing his own anxiety. That was his way of insulating himself from the discomfort of the whole thing. It wasn't the best way, no. But he had no other way. He needed the platitudes.

I really can't judge that. I can't judge a guy on his first lap. He's learning to cope with the way he copes.

Of course, his daughter's needs were bigger. She needed the room to talk, to vent, to get mad. But I figured that the dad was shutting down his daughter because the dad himself had been shut down. My guess is that nobody had given him the room to grieve, either.

I get it. I get why we bury grief. I get why we're told to *move on* and *let go* and *turn the* page. Grief is absolutely terrifying. The brain can't comprehend a thing like that. Mortality is unbearable. You have to see me go or I have to see you go. It's a really bad deal. The terror of it is enough to keep you up a while.

There's no school for this sort of thing. We're conditioned to cheer each other up. Nobody knows what to do with inevitability. A person in denial, who uses religious clichés and says, "Don't cry" and all that sort of tough guy talk, is usually just scared out of his mind. That's his way of dancing around the terror. No one can stand looking into the maw of death, the void of no way back, without their hairs standing up. Most of us have to whistle-and-cartwheel past the graveyard. We're told that if we can say the right combination of magic words, then pain can be solved like a math problem. So most of us have to wax poetic and end up offering all kinds of crass and clumsy buzzwords. I can't blame anyone. We rush past the abyss because the abyss is rushing toward us all. We find clichés because they're usually the only branches to grab on the way down.

Before I'm too hard on anybody about their one-liners, I have to pause. *This is the best that he's got right now. It's not great, but he's trying.*

— — —

Can you do me a favor? In fact, I need this from you. You probably need this from me.

Give me room to scream. To scream at the anguish of loss. To scream until it makes you uncomfortable. I know you want to fix it, or say something deep and profound, or try to bow-tie the whole thing. Who wouldn't? You and I are scavengers for silver linings. Even bronze ones. And I know that's because you have the purest of intentions, and you would feel helpless just letting me fall into a heap. I'm sure your advice is good, but your advice is not as good as being on the floor with me. To catch me, if you have to. There's a time for words later. There will be a time for burgers and dumb movies and loud music, for losing at bowling, drinking hot cocoa, bringing your dog to my place, and for casseroles I will never finish. Right now, though, I just need you to be around through the worst of it. Through the pure hurt of it.

There's no theology that will make this better. But maybe you're the miracle I've been praying for.

AUNTIE, A DEATH WEDDING: A GOODBYE RITUAL

During my residency, my wife's aunt went into hospice care—so we held a funeral for her right in front of her.

She had breast cancer and she was ready to die. We flew to Texas to be with her. The entire family was there: siblings, cousins, children, a room of thirty-something people. A Maltese puppy sat on my aunt-in-law's lap. The puppy's name was Sarang, the Korean word for love.

Each of the family, in turn, got to say something to my aunt-in-law. We said the things we would have said for a eulogy. Or for a wedding. How she cared for us. The kindness and goodness she had shown in life. Those peculiar oddities of a person's being: their home, their habits, the inside jokes and catchphrases.

We sang hymns. We even laughed. My aunt-in-law read Psalm 139 in a shaking voice. She was able to thank every person in the room. She blessed our marriages, our children, our futures. As painful as it was, she tried her best to hug every person there.

Three weeks later, she was gone.

— — —

What I remember from her pre-funeral service is that many of our family members took pictures. Even videos. They replayed the videos at dinner time, a bunch of us slobbering over each other like the worst party ever, tears for confetti and IV bags for balloons. At first, I thought the photos and videos were inappropriate. But that's the kind of people we are. We archive. We're strong on heritage. Our lineage and ancestors are important. I've seen similar things in the bereavement room of many Eastern families: they will take videos of the dying and the dead. They want to remember.

Nearly every other group in the world has a direct *death engagement* where grief is a way of life. These are not new traditions. Each year, Koreans celebrate deathdays. We have a special service where we read a timeline of the deceased together; my father-in-law has a laminated record of his late father's achievements. We share anything we may have learned from them. The extended family is expected to meet at the same time every year for this service.[3]

Maybe that sounds unhealthy to you. Having a pre-funeral or a deathday is not in any kind of textbook. And I'm not sure it's okay for everyone. But who's to say that *moving on* is right, anyway? Who am I to tell somebody to forget? I have seen over and over the healing power of remembering. Of honoring. Of keeping the dead in our stories.

Certain things they should stay the way they are.
You ought to be able to stick them in one of those big glass cases
and just leave them alone.

—J. D. SALINGER, *THE CATCHER IN THE RYE*[4]

I don't remember what my aunt-in-law told me. I'm sure I could watch the video again. What I remember is the way she held my hand and looked me fully in the face. How her love coursed like a waterfall, and we were both nearly laughing through tears. I felt she was giving her life to us. It's rare to connect that way. It's rare to share so purely in the widest range of our sadness and stories and our torn-open chests.

Saying goodbye wasn't a matter of moving on like I had thought it was. It was about letting the other person's story settle into mine, merging, joining, enlarging, weaving. Saying goodbye, I've learned, is the opposite of moving on. It's to bring their story fully into mine, into yours.

Grief, it seems, is less about letting go and more about letting in.

This is what I mean. When my friend John died on my assigned floor, five days after an accident, somebody told me, "We can keep his legacy alive." I had thought *legacy* was a lofty word, a big idea for inventors and explorers. But it's not like that. Out of anybody I've ever known, I want to keep John's legacy alive. The way he was so interested in everything that everyone did. How he always had a silly, sheepish, almost embarrassed grin. How he would always text me a quote he liked, or a podcast he heard, or an insight he had at six in the morning. Or how in all seriousness, he asked me after he heard me preach, "Why aren't you famous?"

I laughed really hard then. But he didn't. To him, everybody was famous. He saw stars all day long. I wanted that sort of earnestness, his sincerity. I wanted, and still want, to see like he did.

I'd like to think that even after somebody is gone, you can keep carrying their voice, the parts you loved, the parts you miss, the parts that God bestowed as a gift for the allotted time they were around.

I know that people have told you to *let go*. I suppose there's a healthy way to do that. But I'm keeping John alive. I can't forget him. I won't.

I'm telling you, you don't have to let it all go. You can hold on. The people you lost, the dreams you had, the secrets and promises you shared: they were for you. Their voice builds into yours. Their voices carry on.

But now we can summon the memories of them at will . . . they seem almost as integral to our being as our skin, or as a comfortable robe we wrap ourselves in at the end of a busy and tiring day. A loved one—a memory to be with, a quiet companion.
—MARTHA W. HICKMAN, *HEALING AFTER LOSS*[5]

HE'S AS MAD AS YOU

Grief, at the bottom of it, is angry. It's a response of outrage. It's an admission that loss is not right. Grief must weep because grief is refusal. It is defiance and rebellion. It pushes back against entropy.

The most surprising verse in Scripture, to me, is also the shortest. It's about grief. You probably know it.

the voices we carry

Jesus wept.

Jesus wept over His dead friend Lazarus. I mean, seconds later Jesus woke up the guy. But Jesus was still mad about it. He could have told the people, "First of all, I'm the Son of God. Second of all, see first of all." He doesn't do that. He's mad. Mad about death. Mad that we die. That little verse—*Jesus wept*—means that He gets it. He knows this isn't how it's supposed to be.

This brings a lot of comfort to me. I mean it. Amidst the hundreds of dead and dying I've seen, this is sometimes the only thing that gets me through. I have to believe that God is shaking His fist, too. That He grieves with us. That He is just as mad as we are about the whole thing. That He loves us enough to weep.

Grief tells me that nobody should go in the ground. Nobody should go in a box. Nobody should be forgotten. Somebody tells me to move on, I'm telling them to get out. Somebody tries to take my grief—well, just try. I'm never going to forget. I'm never going to get over it. I will keep living, but I will always keep the dead with me.

The cross tells us something about Jesus being in our pain, being with us all the way. He isn't far from the hospital bed. He isn't a stranger to long-gone dreams. And then there's the story. In an empty garden, there is resurrection. Futures don't end in a box. And hope is not a dream, but *a memory of the future.*

C. S. Lewis wrote, "Nothing is yet in its true form."[6] I believe that. I believe that in the embrace of the resurrection story, all this loss, this trauma, these unfulfilled longings, will be healed by our home that awaits.

Until then, we wait. We will have to say goodbye for a while. It's the cost of living. The cost of loving. Some days will feel as

204

upside-down as Friday. But I believe we will meet again. I believe I will see you there on Sunday—and I believe it will be like we had never been gone at all.

I want to believe that so badly.

I will see you again.

> *And God shall wipe away all tears from their eyes;*
> *and there shall be no more death,*
> *neither sorrow, nor crying,*
> *neither shall there be any more pain:*
> *for the former things are passed away.*
> —JOHN, THE LETTER OF REVELATION[7]

HOPE IS ONE DAY: ON THE DREAMBOAT RIVER

They're all dead. But in a story, which is a kind of dreaming,
the dead sometimes smile and sit up and return to the world.
— TIM O'BRIEN, *THE THINGS THEY CARRIED*[8]

I have this other dream that I'm rowing down a river, and on both sides I can see all the dead—and they're okay.

I see Brian and Ryan. I saw both of them in the same shift; one had cancer and one had been in a car accident. They were both in their thirties. They had died nearly the same time. I was paged for both of them. Brian had just gotten married. Ryan had a wife and two kids. Brian was hardly a hundred pounds, and Ryan's femur was showing through a four-inch gash. Their wives talked about Brian and Ryan for hours. Brian's wife had planned on going to

Disney World for their honeymoon. Ryan's wife told me they were trying for a third child.

In my dream, Brian is holding a baby stroller and he's wearing a Mickey Mouse cap. Ryan is with his third child, a smiling son. Brian never had cancer. Ryan had missed that drunk driver. Would you believe it, they're waving at me. It's ridiculous, I know. But with the sunlight thrown across them, they're waving at me.

I see Sonny. He had "failure to thrive" and he kept having seizures. A year before he was admitted, he had woken up to his wife who had died in the middle of the night. It was a tiny tumor they had never known about in her brain. For months, Sonny couldn't sleep or eat. His seizures began in the sixth month. The next one, a very soft one, would kill him.

There he is on the bank, Sonny and his wife, her name was Miranda, and they're waving at me, too, and their dog Bowden is with them, a happy boxer, and it's crazy but he's waving his paw, and Sonny says, *Chap, this is Miranda, who I was telling you about, my Miranda. She's as pretty as I said, right?* I tell him, *Right. You were right.*

Across from Sonny and Miranda and Bowden are two twins. I never knew their names. Their mother, Missy, had given birth to twins who didn't make it. Missy's uterus also had to be removed. I remember them because Missy asked me to pray over her children who would never have a future, and she asked me to baptize her babies, who were still so warm, and I remember that day because I locked myself in a restroom and cried for an hour.

But there they are, the two twins, and I have this idea that their names are Misty and Josie, and they're wearing bright pink dresses and they're surrounded by sunflowers and they're waving too, just like the hundreds of other people along the riverbed, and they're telling me, *Thank you for looking after Mom.*

On one side of the river, I see my friend Grace, dancing. She died of a terminal illness before she turned thirty. We had thrown a prom for her in her hospital room. She is dancing with Sean, a friend we both knew from church, who was killed defending his family when he was a senior in high school. I see Irene's husband Ian, and in one hand he's holding a baked ham, in the other two dozen roses large enough to fill my boat.

The people don't stop. The dead are so many. Some of them, I see their old wounds zipping up as I row past them. I dream them back to wholeness. Scars blinking out, cars missing by inches, bones stitched together, bullets falling in mid-air, the cancer lifting up and out to somewhere else, another universe where cells divide the right way, where holes aren't left by two-pound tumors, where gaps aren't left in picture frames.

I keep rowing gently and the dead come out of the edges of the grass, from the sides of daisies and corn stalks and strange green and blue flowers I've never seen before, and they're all waving trying to tell me they're together and they're okay.

I see my older sister. The one I never had, the one who was aborted before me. I know that it's her. She hoots and hollers and gives me two thumbs up, and I can see her mouth the words, *Hey little brother. You stink.* She laughs, and I wave back.

I see my wife's aunt. She is beautiful. No more gauze or tubes or tears. She's wearing a *hanbok*, a traditional Korean dress, yellow and lavender and green, and one hand is over her smile so wide she can hardly hide it, and her other hand is waving up and down, the Korean style wave, and she tells me, *Be good to my sister. Be good to your wife, like you promised me.*

I think I see John, his sheepish grin, his boyish face poking over a row of violets, his blond locks as bright as everything around us—and I don't want to leave this place.

Then I see Henrietta Ransom, and I try to get out of the boat. I want to tell her that I'm sorry I never got to say goodbye.

She says, *Goodness, I'm fine, chap, can't you see? We're fine here.*

Ms. Ransom, I say, *am I dreaming? Is this real?*

Yes, she says, and she removes her cannula and throws her oxygen tank into the river and stands tall and the years fall out of her face.

The dreams that don't come to pass are as real as the ones that do, she tells me.

What does that mean? I ask her.

It means that nobody has to die, if you dream of them. It means that God has quite a memory, and that's what love is. To love is to remember. Am I talking crazy?

No, I tell her, so relieved to hear her voice. *You're not talking crazy, Rietta.*

I'm out of the boat and my feet fall deep into the water and I see Rietta reach out, and she whispers something but I don't hear what she says. The dead look at me and they're still waving, and I want to hold on to Rietta, I want to hold on to this, I want to stay here with all the people I used to know. With all my patients. They were my friends. I loved them. I want to say something meaningful to Rietta, but I can't think of anything.

Finally, I can only think to say, *I'm sorry. I'm sorry. I would take this all from you. I would take it all if I could.*

I start to wake up, but I can hear Rietta say, *Don't be sorry. Be wonderful for your short little while. Be wonderful.*

— — —

I'm home. It's been a long shift.

I have to do it again the next day.

I fall into a chair and I pray. I pray for these families. Their children. My friends. I think about the river of memories cut short. I wonder if we ever really get enough time. I am mad. I am weeping. I'm full of doubt. Full of panic. Full of fear. My chest is a tightened mess of steel wires and busted rope.

My wife walks in like she does, not turning on a light, knowing when I have a hard day. We hold hands across the table. She gives me room.

I look at my wife. She looks at me. I know the look. I have seen that look of kindness, of strength, in so many wives and mothers and daughters and sisters as they held on to each other, walking one another through a crater. I had seen God in their faces, just as I saw God in my wife's face, too. Even in the dark, I can see her. I'm so glad to see her. I will always see her.

I do my best to smile and I tell her, *"Hello, babe. Thank you for everything."*

Thank you for this short little while.

PART 3

Finding Your Voice

Finding Your Voice

Here's where we are. With this final section, we're going to answer three essential questions:

How much have I been swayed and deceived by lies?
How do I break through the deception to find my own voice?
How do I use my voice to lift up the voices of others, especially those who have been silenced?

Our voices, in the end, are not just to battle and manage. They're also meant to form a *voice of our own*, to serve the people around us and create something good. If you ask me, it's what we're made to do.

— — —

I have to tell you this story.

In a grocery store once, a stranger made an obvious racial insult toward me. A good Samaritan nearby jumped in and immediately came to my defense. She asked, "Why would you say that?" The other person was stunned. So was I. I've been insulted plenty of times in public, but this is the only time I can remember that someone advocated for me.

The woman who spoke up for me really only asked a question, but it was a big deal to step in that way. She spoke a clear message into the world. Maybe she was afraid. Maybe she would've been berated too. But she jumped in anyway. She was compelled. She was determined. Everybody else in that grocery store had a voice too—but this good Samaritan chose to use hers. She spoke life into mine. It's a sad situation that I would even need somebody this way. I guess I could've spoken up for myself. But that's the thing. The reality of it is that I would not have been heard another way. A voice unto itself can be strong, but two together is something else. That's when magic happens.

I've wondered how she could do something like that. For somebody to even have the presence of mind to stick up for me, to have the clarity of vision that says, *I will speak up for good as clearly as I can,* doesn't come around by accident. That's what we're going to discover in the closing pages of this book. We're going to remove the fog from our voices, because they're more hazy than we think. We're going to crystallize our voices, to use them for good, to speak truth into trying situations. If you've ever been silenced, or failed to speak, or you're not always sure what you're really about: I'm with you.

CHAPTER 10

Hearing Voices: Unscrambling the Noise

Wading through a Sea of Everyone Else's Ideas

"So do not be taken in. Pay attention to yourself."
—THE DESERT FATHERS[1]

YOU GOT A PLAN?

Over the intercom, I heard, "Attention staff"—and I waited for the usual code.

But instead, I heard, "Active shooter alert. Repeat, there is an active shooter. Current location unknown."

I was in the middle of a patient visit. Keilah was in a medically induced coma, and her boyfriend Helio had asked for a chaplain. Helio was telling me about a job interview he had in an hour.

"An active shooter?" he said, glancing at the open door. "Is that different than a passive shooter?"

"No, Helio. I guess passive would be better."

He laughed, but only a little. "You got a plan?"

"The protocol is to run, hide, or fight."

"You serious?" he said. "Sounds like my autobiography."

"You've had some practice then, huh?" Helio didn't laugh that time. "Sorry," I said. I started sweating. "We're supposed to barricade the doors and turn off the lights."

"Chap," Helio said, not moving off the recliner, "I'm going to miss my interview, aren't I? It's just across the street, do you think I should—"

"Helio, I need your help," I said. "The recliner is the biggest thing here besides the bed. Let's roll it over to block the door. After that I can call the place where you have the interview, I can tell them what's happening."

"Honestly, chap," Helio said, "I didn't really want that job."

"Huh?"

"So like, if we're going to die in here," he said, still not moving, "I'm thinking now that I don't want this job. I don't want my *life*, actually." Helio blinked slowly. He was part of the chair now. Helio had merged with the vinyl. He was a statue. He looked like he could plant a garden and wait for it to blossom.

"Our chances of dying are very low," I said. I was making small talk, if you can believe it. "Extremely low," I added.

The hallway lights turned off. I could hear footsteps scattering outside the door. I heard a nurse whisper loudly, "Here, in here." I heard more footsteps, then a door shutting. I heard panicked breathing from the nurse's station down the hall, more doors opening and closing. I could hear my heart pounding hard, real hard. I scrambled to close our door and turn off the lights.

I turned back to Helio. "This is a situation. We're in a bad situation."

He didn't see me. He was looking at the floor, at his imaginary garden.

I tried another way. "Helio, I'm sorry about your job interview. I'm sorry that—"

"It's not the interview," he said. He put his head in his hands and started sobbing. "It's my life, man, *my life*, I've wasted it really bad. If I die in here, who cares? *I was so busy living what everybody else wanted that I never got to live.* What a waste, man."

In the silence, besides Helio's sobbing, I heard the elevator ding down the hall. I wasn't sure if people were trying to leave— or if somebody was about to come out the doors.

"Active shooter," the intercom said, *"on the fourth floor."*

That was our floor.

"Helio," I said, bending down to his eye level, "Helio. Look, I'm real sorry. I think I get it. I've done so much that I regret. I didn't do a lot of things I should've done, too. Everybody spends time trying to live everybody else's vision. We all do that. But it's not a waste. You just found out what you didn't like. Process of elimination, you know?"

"You're going to use the word *elimination* right now?"

"Sorry, poor choice," I said. "Helio, it's not over yet. Your life, I mean. It might be five more seconds or fifty more years, but it's not over yet. You can still be who you're going to be. Can you help me?"

He looked up. "Fine, fine" he said. "Inspire me so I can get off the chair, huh?" But Helio stood up. I unlocked the chair and we rolled it to the door.

We both crouched in front of Keilah. Without saying it, I knew that Helio would cover her body if it came to that.

We waited thirty minutes. We didn't talk much during the waiting. There was only Keilah's rhythmic breathing through her vent. At some point, Helio and I sat on the ground and leaned against the bed, knees up to our chest.

Finally, the intercom made a beep. "Attention, attention. Please dismiss the previous alert. False alarm, everyone. False alarm." The lady over the intercom made a long *phew*, but she realized she was still on. She turned off her mic in the middle of her *phew* noise. For a minute, there was an eerie vacuum of quiet. Soon, I heard doors opening.

"That's it, huh?" Helio said.

"No sweat," I said, wiping the sweat off my eyelids. "Do you want me to call that employer?"

"Hmm," Helio said. He shook his head. "Thank you, but no. I think this is the moment that I go a new way. It's so dumb that I had to wait for something like this, isn't it? This is the fork in the road where I make something of myself. How's that for my autobiography?"

"What would you call this chapter?" I asked him.

"Finding My True Voice. Subtitle: Throwing Out the False People That I Tried to Be."

> *I wondered what I had been using for brains all my life.*
> — PHILIP MARLOWE, *FAREWELL, MY LOVELY*[2]

I have to tell you the truth. That story isn't exactly true. I mean,

218

Helio really did miss a job interview because of a false active shooter alert, and he really was Keilah's boyfriend, and he really was ready to cover her body. But I wasn't in the room.

Helio told me his story the next day when I went to visit him. He wanted me to get inside his headspace, for me to feel what he felt. He kept saying, "Imagine you're me, you're in this room, stuck and waiting to die." He added, "That was like a metaphor for my actual life. Weird thing is, being in that room, coming up with a plan to live: that was the *one time* I ever had a plan for myself."

He was relieved that he missed the job interview. And he really did say, *I was so busy living what everybody else wanted that I never got to live.*

"Hacky, isn't it?" Helio said. "A really hacky movie line."

No, I told him. I liked it. I liked it just fine.

EVERYBODY'S GOT A VISION FOR YOUR LIFE

It seems that in the hospital, I was hearing that sort of thing all the time. Patients questioned their own purpose, their plot, their reason for being. You get to the dying part of your life and it tends to make you think about what your life was about.

I know, the idea of *your one precious and wild life* is so gushy and sincere, it's enough to get your eyes rolling. But one after another, dying people would tell me they had been living someone else's vision for them. They were living their precious life in the service of others' voices. Sometimes that life was a mystery stew, compiled from unknown meats and road kill. Or they had tried to please some family member or inner circle, and those people would leave anyway. The saddest thing to me was when they had been pulled along all the while by random ideas, pushed around by neon signs, their lives *persuaded* onto the next exit, with no continuity.

— — —

All of us, at some level or another, have bought into a vision without question. Every one of us have formed a particular **base-line narrative**—a story about how things work—adopted from a mishmash of history, family, religion, culture, and all the things that happened to us. That narrative also gets jammed up with all the advice and opinions you hear day-to-day, a sludge of philosophies tucked deeply into your brain-folds. It's not a matter of *if* we're buying into a particular narrative. It's a matter of which one.

Some of the time, we're aware of what we intend to do and why, but a lot of the time, we act out of something already set deep in our bones. There are the things we say we believe, but then there's what we really do—and very often, they're two different things. Or as psychologist Timothy Wilson says, often *"we are strangers to ourselves."*[3]

There's some research that explains this is how most behavior works: you have a *conscious self* that's aware of what you're doing, and an *automatic self* filled with patterns, prejudices, and socialized norms.[4] I know this is a bit of an overused metaphor, but it works: imagine the tip of an iceberg as your conscious self, and the rest of the iceberg as your automatic self, hidden from view. Your automatic self tends to spontaneously act on a patchwork of conditioned responses. In the split second between motive and action, it can pull the strings, firing off a reflex, unleashing a strange cough that's been lodged up in your guts. Like a wind-up toy, you can launch into some unexpected place you had never planned on. Even when you attempt to make conscious choices, your automatic self will still try to keep you in its grip, reverting to your comfortable baseline.[5]

This means that your automatic self is always fighting to be in charge. You'll know this is true when 1) you're confused about what you do all the time, sort of like the way I look at the mall, and 2) you have to constantly justify your behavior afterward. This will lead you to reinforce patterns that are not good for you, leading to more confusion. Your automatic self gets hidden even further. This gets you *stuck in an unexamined life you never wanted.*

Here's the good news. You *can* get to know the stranger in your brain. You can draw out all those ugly, unconscious patterns. Then you can find better ones to follow, and you can finally align your conscious self with your automatic self. So you'll not only know *what* you're deciding, but *why.*

When you can better understand the choices you make, you'd not only make better choices, but you'd have more confidence in your ability to choose.[6] Research has shown that this sort of congruence brings a higher sense of well-being and satisfaction.[7] In other words, *the more you know yourself, the more at peace you'll be with who you are and what you do.* The examined life will stand on something and will know why it's standing there. It belongs to you. It will bring awareness, clarity, and curiosity, *with one hand open to receive new ideas and one hand closed for the person you will not compromise.*

The thing is, it's hard to flush out all your hidden stuff. Your automatic self is a mixed up cauldron of a thousand different voices all at once. But, *your automatic self is not impossible to know and to change.* It's possible to no longer be a stranger to yourself. You can find a real voice that isn't just a reflex or reaction or cobbled from spare parts, but a deliberate voice built from the things you choose and the things that are really you.

THE BIGGEST PICTURE

My mother used to tell me that I had an *easy ear.* I tend to believe everything that everybody is saying all the time. I'm easily swayed. For example, I accidentally joined a cult once. I didn't plan on it, but they were saying nice things until months later, I looked around and realized, "Okay, this is a cult. I'm in a cult."

For a guy like Helio and a guy like me, we had bought into our groupthink wholesale. We did what we were told, good little boys inheriting the family business, toeing the company line, nodding along to everyone else's drum. I'm certain that even the rebellious stuff I had done was still a type of mindless conformity. A life lived that way, out of reaction to everyone else, is sort of an anti-life. It has no originating force, no engine. It doesn't know what it's about.

That isn't necessarily anyone's fault, by the way, but it doesn't have to be our fate, either. If we're to have a strong vision for our lives, to not have such an easy ear, it requires first deconstructing the things we believe and why we believe them.

In the landmark work *Sapiens,* anthropologist Yuval Noah Harari has a name for the narratives we believe: he calls them *imagined orders* or *fictions.* He says these fictions are not all bad. We need made-up institutions like banks, traffic lights, painted lines on a road, contracts, governments, and the little plastic bar that separates groceries at checkout, all to organize us at a larger level. We need unseen ideas like traditions and norms to insert meaning and structure. Without these fictions, we'd get social madness. Harari writes,

> **The imagined order shapes our desires** ... Every person is born into a pre-existing imagined order, and his or her desires are shaped from birth by its dominant myths. Our personal desires thereby become the imagined order's most important defences.[8]

Harari might go so far as to say that nothing we believe is original. For example, about the phrase, "Follow your heart," he says:

> Friends giving advice often tell each other, "Follow your heart." But the heart is a double agent that usually takes its instructions from the dominant myths of the day, and the very recommendation to "Follow your heart" was implanted in our minds by a combination of nineteenth-century Romantic myths and twentieth-century consumerist myths.[9]

These fictions, unfortunately, add a *bias* to all the ways we perceive the world. You know the old saying:

We do not see things as they are,
we see them as we are.[10]

When our narratives go unchecked, this bias can do at least two things:

1. Lock us into certain beliefs
2. Lock us into a group that reinforces those beliefs

One of the most powerful things about a narrative is that it can gather a cluster of like-minded individuals and bond them like nothing else. Each person in the group can enable the other person exponentially. This can be a good thing. This is how change happens on the widest scale. The problem is that it can isolate us into a self-affirming silo.

A group like this, sometimes called an *in-group*,[11] might wear the same dress and move in straight lines, fueled by the fear of excommunication, but it's not always so obvious. The most dangerous groups have you *wanting* to follow the rules. They will continually cheerlead you as you follow the secret rules and subroutines, locking you in a Pavlovian dopamine cycle.[12] A like-minded group is very appealing. As we learned in chapter 5, a group can form by trying to "fix the universe" or some other noble idea. And it feels great to get inside with the insiders. They'll be your best friends, *if.* Your beliefs—*their* beliefs—are championed by a chanting choir. The chant is, *One of us.*

That's how you get pulled in. You can get won over by yes-men yessing each other. You can get seduced by the promise of belonging. It's a dastardly scheme. It's a scheme that works.

You might think you're not so quick to fall for something like this, but you only need to look at the things you read online. Most of us are prone to read the things that already confirm our beliefs. That's called *confirmation bias,* which is powered by *motivated reasoning.*[13] We're likely to block out certain information that contradicts "the way things are." You end up spellbound in the Chamber of Echoes. Even a club of tough guys who simultaneously yell, "I do what I want" only need to look left and right to see the irony. And while it's nice to be cheered on sometimes, if you ever decide to question your group, you're likely to be called a traitor. To question your group is anathema. Disagreement is smothered and stomped out.

I have to tell you that groups are not bad. A narrative is not bad. Rules and rituals are not bad. We need them. But they need examination. They need accountability. A healthy community will allow questions, will disagree, will challenge their own practices, and will have the courage and compassion to speak up to their leaders. Healthy persons will also question themselves, disagree with themselves, examine their own ideas, and speak up to their own ways. With healthy places and people, there will be channels which allow a way to inspect their operations.

What does that even look like?

THAT'S SOME GOOD DETECTIVE WORK

The way through all these different voices is a word you might have heard before: *discernment.* You rotate an idea to see every angle, to examine the infrastructure, use a microscope and an X-ray and a fine-tooth comb, and filter out the good and bad of it. Like Aristotle said: "It is the mark of an educated mind to be able to entertain a thought without accepting it."[14]

Discernment opens up dialogue, whether with others or ourselves, to dissect the things we believe in and where we hear them from.[15] In moments where you think you're hearing a bad idea, you can ask some gentle questions. These are not new questions, but sometimes a charming idea can make you forget to ask them.

It's worth your time to ask these four things:

1. Where did you hear that?
2. What does [that term] mean to you?
3. Why do you believe it to be true?
4. How has it worked out for you?

1. *Where did you hear that?*

Says who? On whose authority? What makes this source credible?

2. *What does [that term] mean to you?*

Are we using the same definitions? When you say ____, what do you mean?

3. *Why do you believe it to be true?*

What led you to this belief? What about alternative ideas? How would you argue from the other side of things?

4. *How has it worked out for you?*

What is the logical conclusion of this idea? How has it helped you? How has it not helped you? Is this something you would teach your friend or your children?

Maybe this looks like overthinking, but here's why this is important: Some of our beliefs are harmful. The stakes are too high to let them go unexamined. The wrong sort of idea can impede the course of a life. Some beliefs will quietly, but most assuredly, consume us. Some of them need a good talking to.

This patient Natalia told me she had lost her husband in a car wreck, but as bad as that was, she told me, "My pastor said I just have to accept it. He said I can't get mad at God. He told me if I get mad, then I'll go to hell." Natalia was already in a bad spot, *but her beliefs were an extra burden she had to carry.* Seeing Natalia there, crushed by her pastor's words, I felt immense sadness and anger. I saw myself too. Do you see yourself there? Have you been told similar things?

I met a lot of patients like this, afflicted by beliefs that could affect their recovery. I don't mean to say that if they believed the "right thing" that they would get better. I mean to say there are bad ideas that could make them worse. Many of our beliefs *add a burden* rather than *relieve the burden.* When a patient tells me, "I just need to stay positive," or "God is punishing me right now," those sorts of beliefs are an extra plate to spin on an already shaky plate-spinning situation. More than that, the unwavering conviction to those ideas, without really investigating them, can drive a person mad, to ruin.

I wanted to tell Natalia that what her pastor said was hogwash—but that's not what chaplains do, and besides, if some chaplain had tried to tell *me* that I was all mixed up, I might have shown them the door, or a window. It's because *our precious beliefs are viciously and dearly held, even when they harm us.* They're severely ingrained, an essential stitch in our being. How do you unravel such a harmful thing without unraveling the rest of the brain?

In the end, I've learned that nobody else can challenge those beliefs but yourself. In the silence, between you and God, there has to be an unpleasant reckoning. It's a tricky thing, even nause-ating, to challenge what you and I believe. But some beliefs *have* to be challenged.

I GOT QUESTIONS AND I WANT ANSWERS

In a church service I attended long ago, a pastor gave a message subtitled "A Faith of Your Own." Near the end, the pastor said, "But don't believe anything I'm saying. I mean, how do you know that I'm not lying to you right now? You don't need me. You don't need a preacher to tell you what the Bible says. Thank God for scholars and seminaries, but there's no secret insider informa-tion. It's all here. You can open up this book and have a faith for yourself. Think for yourself. Don't inherit your parents' faith. Don't trust me. Don't trust every eloquent college professor. Bloggers are not experts. Question everyone. *And please think critically for yourself.*"[16]

He told us that our brains were clever enough to deceive us, but also smart enough to see through the deception.

That message stuck with me. His concern was that each of us were unwittingly building a piecemeal personality of random quotes and philosophers and YouTubers without thinking through these things. He reminded us that we already had the tools to look inside and interrogate our biases, blind spots, and harmful beliefs.

— — —

One of the things I believe about my faith is that we're called to put everything to the test. Paul says, "Do not treat prophecies with contempt but test them all; hold on to what is good, reject every kind of evil."[17] When he says prophecies, he's talking about teachings from people who claimed to speak for God. Paul says they're not all bad, but they need to be tested the same way we test money or metal. Luke tells us about the Berean people, who had *readiness of mind* and cross-checked Paul to see if Paul was for real.[18]

All throughout Scripture, the famous Bible figures are always doubting God or interrogating God or testing God or inexplicably ripping their shirts and covering their heads in burlap bags and saying dramatic things like, "Look on me and answer, LORD my God. Give light to my eyes, or I will sleep in death."[19] They felt free to rant, to demand an explanation. A guy like Job shakes his fist for thirty-something chapters and rolls around on the floor a lot. Then God comes along in a hurricane and sort of says, "All right Job, I know you're mad, but here's the thing." I never see God saying, "Okay, you stop that" or anything. He takes their complaints seriously and is open to their questions. Then God offers other ideas and challenges their dearly held notions.

Too many places, whether church, social media, a college campus, a workplace, or a political party don't allow you to think for yourself, be yourself, or question anybody else. If you did, it would end in social death. But I believe God is open to our openness. At the heartbeat of the universe is a welcome sign that says, *I've been around a while, so ask me anything.* That's the sort of God who takes the burdens off, not puts them on. I believe He exists outside of our eras and opinions and philosophies and holds a sort of timeless wisdom, a kind of wisdom that isn't necessarily about *what* to think, but *how*. He calls us to pay attention, to discern.

This a personal idea for me. I wish some churches and businesses and online groups I had been a part of were more skeptical of their own practices. If they had been, they might have been more accountable to the ways they hurt people. I might have had the confidence to say, "We're open to new ideas no matter where they come from," or "What we're doing right now is wrong and it will never, ever happen again." I have always thought the best institutions were ones that were the most skeptical of their own ideas while at the same time the gentlest with the people inside. I imagine that healthy places would have outsiders saying, *I'm not worried about them, because they're always keeping themselves in check.*

You know you're in a good place when people can say, *I was wrong, I'm sorry, and I want to know how to do better,* and others believe it. You find yourself open to questioning yourself and listening to others more. You find yourself expanding.

A WORD FOR YOU:

Think It Through and Get Back to Me.
Sincerely, Brain

Somebody told me once that we all need a *balcony moment*. That's when you get on a balcony and think for a while on what you're doing and where you're going. I don't mean that you sit around all day looking out a window. I mean, you test yourself, doing some detective work on your own guts.

Have you done that sort of thing before? I wish I had done it earlier. You need a balcony moment once in a while to clear the cobwebs. It's easy to get lost in the buzz of routine, the fast city lights and all. You look across the way one morning and realize you're a passive participant in the world you're steeped in.

So would you do this? For a few days or so, don't listen to any podcasts or read any blogs. Don't check anybody's social media to read their take on the latest headline. Step back from all the invisible laws of your church and workplace and online community. Spend some time in silence or meditation or prayer or with a notepad. Ask yourself all the questions. And when you come back to the world of voices around you, see if something has changed.

I think you'll be surprised. I think you'll come back with a sober mind. A new set of ears and eyes. You'll look at some of your favorite authors and bloggers and speakers and see that their catchphrases are nice and said with good intentions, but some of them don't hold up. A few of their ideas were wrapped inside a magical spell of eloquence and humor that had nothing real on the inside. You'll see that their view, and yours, was just *one interpretation* of the world and not a world that you should wholly buy into.

You might be disturbed at how quickly some of your beliefs fall apart. Like I said, it could get nauseating. It'll be quite a kick in the head. There are plenty of ideas you hold that are wax scaffolding, and they'll melt under the slightest heat of scrutiny. But there's a mercy in this. You'll get free of some bad ideas. You'll be less likely to get caught by them too. You'll get vaccinated against deception.[20] You can swish around an idea for a while, until you can safely keep it or discard it. And the things you decide to keep will become tangible and a deeper part of you.

So I'm begging you, *please don't trust me*. Please don't trust a witty, articulate-sounding person just because they have a lot of fans and fancy language. Do the due diligence. Replace second-guessing with double-checking. Double-check and gut-check. Be a gumshoe. Do the detective work.

— — —

Somewhere down the line, the questioning and cross-examining can't go on forever. As fun as it is, we can't keep asking, "Says who? Based on what? Why should I?" Like C. S. Lewis says, "You cannot go on 'seeing through' things for ever. The whole point of seeing through something is to see something through it."[21]

It's true. I don't think that every idea is an "imagined order" or a "fiction" that we just make up to pass the time. I believe those imagined orders and fictions emerged from something real. In this we find a real voice, a voice calling us into being, speaking us into the people we're meant to be.

Here's where you find a voice of your own.

CHAPTER 11

Owning Your Voice(s): What You're Really About

Finding a Voice to Call Your Own

Everybody is original, if he tells the truth, if he speaks from himself.
But it must be from his true self and not from the self he thinks
he should be.

—BRENDA UELAND, *IF YOU WANT TO WRITE*[1]

I was talking with Chaplain Rebecca. She had described herself as a recovering people-pleaser. She told me that during a one-on-one, her supervisor had asked her a simple question:

Who is Rebecca?

It was a ridiculous question, one of those philosophical pretzels that you could chuckle at—but Rebecca had no answer. She had tried and tried, and then burst into tears.

"That question was haunting," she told me. "*Who* is Rebecca? Who *is* Rebecca? Who is *Rebecca*? What things does she like?

Maybe more important, what does she *not* like? I had to ask myself, '*Who are you without anybody else?*' How could I stand up for myself if I didn't know what I was standing up for?"

Who are you without them?

Who is ____?

— — —

The theologian Howard Thurman, who was a mentor to Dr. Martin Luther King Jr., talks about the internal conflict this way:

> There are so many noises going on inside of you, so many echoes of all sorts, so many internalizing of the rumble and the traffic, the confusions, the disorders by which your environment is peopled that I wonder if you can get still enough—not quiet enough—still enough to hear rumbling up from your unique and essential idiom the sound of the genuine in you.[2]

And he asks, "What is your name—who are you—and can you find a way to hear **the sound of the genuine** in yourself?"[3]

— — —

Finding your voice, the sound of your genuine, means *finding the story you want to tell, and telling it well.*

This is your message you bring with you and that you hope to speak into the world.

The voice you have, a lot of times, is still composed of other people. The way you write songs or run a meeting or raise children or even the way you talk might have been crowdsourced by a lot of influences. That's a good way to find your own voice, by studying others. But you might also deprive everybody of *your* voice.

I think with all the information around, it's easy to plagiarize an identity without meaning to. And if you're like me, you're likely to run to your favorite expert's opinion. You might fully trust your authorities—your pastor and celebrities and bloggers and podcasts—to do your thinking. These are not bad things. They can be supplements, sure. But to transplant their thoughts and views into your brain is like waiting for somebody's fish instead of learning how to fish on your own.

Besides, each of these people are just people. They're on their own journeys too. They've done the legwork of forming their own opinion—or they haven't, which will leave you in the same basement that they're blogging from.

No matter how much you'd like to, you can't cram somebody's lifetime of wisdom into your brain in hopes that you'll become just as wise. Even if you can parrot back everything they've ever said or written, you'll end up looking like a wordy parrot. The "click" moment you experience during a TED Talk or sermon or book, while a good thing, is not the same thing as believing that epiphany and turning it into action. It's good to be inspired by your favorite people, but it requires that you taste and digest their ideas before you land on a solid conviction. Otherwise you remain a river, when you have the power to be an ocean.

BRING YOURSELF ALONG

In a one-on-one, Audrey handed me a piece of paper. She asked, "What are your **non-negotiables**?"

"Non-negotiables?"

"The *you* that you bring to a room. The values you lift up everywhere you go. What you'd fight for. What you want to bring in. What you never budge from. Basically, *what are you about*?"

I didn't have to think long. I wrote down:

1. *Grace for the stories of others.* To honor the whole story, to empathize with where they came from and where they were going.

2. *Offering justice to injury.* To bring healing into a gap between what *is* and what *ought* to be, in the best way I could, to see people safe and free.

3. *Making a creative space for our voices.* To make room for expression, to promote the creator in every person, to open doors for artistry.

Have you done a thing like this yet? Asked or reminded yourself about the values you carry?

If you do, I can almost promise that you'll walk into a room with more clarity, less fog, more momentum. It'll push back the negative self-talk and a lot of the other voices pulling at you in a hundred different ways.

In fact, *with a genuine voice of your own, other false voices won't take hold so easily.*

A strange study I read was that the act of eating can prevent an advertisement from working on you. That's called *oral interference.* If you watch a commercial and chew gum at the same time, you're less likely to buy into the commercial. The theory goes that if you're eating something, your brain shuts off *subvocalization,* the internal repeating of what you read, hear, and see. Your mouth is already chewing on something, so it can't repeat the commercial that's playing.[4]

What this could mean, spiritually and philosophically speaking, is that if your mouth is already full, you can't chew on other things. In other words, if *you already have a strong internal voice, then other voices are less likely to crowd in on you.*

IN YOUR CHEST ROARS TRUTH

I believe that this strong internal voice is composed of our non-negotiables, our values, set deep in our chests by a real and pure truth. They are nothing we made up ourselves, but must only be discovered.

A pastor I know once told it to me like this: *God made you the way He made you because He wanted to say something through you that He can't through anyone else.* I know that's a bit hard to believe, but it's true. You're meant for something that good.

I didn't have to search long for my non-negotiables, either, because they were not random. I thought of the times I came alive or suffered loss, the times I felt belonging and when that belonging had been taken from me. I was certain looking back that both the holy gifts and hard edges pointed to the values I wanted to bring into every room. Theologian Frederick Buechner says it best:

"The place God calls you to is the place where your deep gladness and the world's deep hunger meet."[5] To me, that means I'm called to bring in the things I wanted to have and didn't always get to. Or as someone once told me: *To bring flowers to a world bereft of beauty.* That's my hope, anyway, for all the places I go.

Before I enter a patient's room at the hospital, while I'm sanitizing at the doorway, I've gotten into the habit of asking a simple question before I enter: *God, how do You want to work through me right now?* And I remember my non-negotiables, the *me* that God has called into being. It's a humbling thing, to know that I get to do this work. To know that I have a voice. To know where it's from.

You're called, too.

It comes the very moment you wake up each morning. All your wishes and hopes for the day rush at you like wild animals. And the first job each morning consists simply in shoving them all back; in listening to that other voice, taking that other point of view, letting that other larger, stronger, quieter life come flowing in. And so on, all day. Standing back from all your natural fussings and frettings; coming in out of the wind.

—C. S. LEWIS, *MERE CHRISTIANITY*[6]

If you've never done it before, I hope you get to write down some non-negotiables, the values you seek and bring.[7] *Yours*, in your God-given voice. You might have already done it, but they're easy to forget. Like Brené Brown says, "In those moments when we start putting other voices in front of our own, we forget what made us go into the arena in the first place, the reason we're there. We forget our values."[8] You need them at the forefront of your vision, propelling you forward.

Here's why this is important. In aviation school, they teach you how to handle emergencies. If you find yourself in a helicopter upside-down in the middle of a snowstorm, the first thing to ask is, *What is my point of reference?* You look for a spot in the sky, or your hip, or the door, to find where you are. It's to steady yourself and to know where to go next.

In our case, when all our critical voices come swooping in, the voices of our parents or trauma or guilt or shipwreck or self-doubt, we need the reference point. Your non-negotiables. And it's from your point of reference that you can begin to manage those other voices, to see if there's truth in them that will help you get better or get unstuck. In fact, there's good stuff to keep from your family and favorite blogger and the stranger you chatted with on the bus. But it begins by solidifying yourself. Then, and only then, can you have the fortitude to toss out what doesn't work. You can step back from the false voices and step back into who you know yourself to be. Back into *your* voice.

I KNOW THE PLANS I HAVE FOR YOU:
A LOT OF WILDERNESS AND CHAPPED LIPS

When you've found your voice, there's good news and bad news.

The good news is, when you figure out the non-negotiables you want to act on, you begin to move in a clarity and freedom that's like nothing else. It's a sweet spot. You don't get displaced so easily, and you make decisions with more conviction. That's all a good place to be.

The bad news is that once you find your voice, you also find that it's hard to make a difference. You hope that it would be enough to speak loudly and stick up for worthwhile things, but the world moves along a comfortable grain that isn't easy to change.

In other words, just like you have a *conscious self* and an *automatic self*, the world around you does too. When you start aligning yourself with the values you want, people and places might push back. You hope your efforts will pay off, but it's rare. Investing "one unit of good works" almost never means you will get back "one unit of ideal outcomes."

A lot of times, finding your voice leads to disillusionment. You get passionate about things, but other people look at your excitement and cough. It can feel like your newfound voice is hollering into a void.

> *More often than not, raising my voice comes at some cost.*
> *... In many ways, giving birth to a child was easier than giving birth*
> *to my voice.*
>
> — KATHY KHANG, *RAISE YOUR VOICE*[9]

This whole thing reminds me of the prophet Jeremiah. When he was a kid, just seventeen, God called him to be a preacher. He tells God, "I cannot speak: for I am a child."[10] But God touches Jeremiah's mouth, which would normally kill a guy, and Jeremiah goes on to preach for forty years.

This sounds like a pretty good deal. But we're told that Jeremiah wasn't allowed to get married or have kids or have friends.[11] I imagine a scene where Jeremiah is looking through a window at people eating and drinking, and he knows he won't ever have that. His church attendance remained zero. It's possible that Jeremiah was so weird and passionate that people kept their distance. I mean, at one point Jeremiah says, "I will make them eat the flesh of their sons and daughters, and they will eat one another's flesh,"[12] which is something I've never heard at a house party. Either way, he walked alone.

Jeremiah has been called the "weeping prophet," which is the worst nickname of all time. He was sad and sick about God's people because of their general destructiveness and disobedience, including his own. A pattern emerges where Jeremiah rebukes the people, and they respond by beating him up or throwing him in shackles or throwing him in a well.[13] I feel a lot of sadness when I think of Jeremiah. I think of his loneliness and my breath catches. I can't comprehend a life of forty years with no one by his side, getting beaten up all the while, thinking it's all a waste, while staying faithful to his mission.

Before Jeremiah dies, he declares a prophecy that the people of God are going to be freed from Babylon. At the time, the Judean people had been kidnapped from their homes and enslaved into the nation of Babylon. I mean, this was sort of the Judean people's fault; they had broken a promise with God, and that's not a thing to take lightly. But Jeremiah essentially tells the Judeans, *I promise you, God is going to bring you back home.* He tells them the name of the emperor who will set them free and even the exact date that it will happen.[14] It seems nobody believes him. Why would they?

According to legend, Jeremiah is killed by a pile of rocks thrown at his head. My guess is that the Judeans finally had it with both his preaching and prophecies. He's reportedly buried in Egypt, miles away from his single bedroom home.

Thirty years later, as Jeremiah predicted, the Judeans are set free.

Here's what I gather: Jeremiah never got to see the fruits of his labor, but he was called for the work. He was given a voice. He was given that prophecy. He preached for the people to repent, to change their hearts and behavior, even after they threw him around. Jeremiah chose to speak, and that choice most likely did him in. But still, he spoke. I'd like to think that Jeremiah, in his boldness, had some kind of impact on the Babylonian emperor and even on God's people, the Judeans. I know it was God who moved them. But I'd like to think that through Jeremiah, those divine seeds were planted. That his voice reverberated, way past himself. Through Jeremiah, God spoke an entirely new timeline into existence. His words became a garden. His words still bear fruit today.

God gives you a voice too. It's your choice to speak.

A WORD FOR YOU:

Easy Come, Hard to Go

My friend, it's quite a thing to own your voice. Especially when you say something different than what everybody else is saying. Then you have a choice. You can leave, and in most cases that would be wise. Or you're called to stay, to be the one voice of change.

I've stayed in unhealthy places much longer than I should have. I thought I could be brave and romantic and change a place like that by *loving them* and saying *yes* all the time. But it was too late for many of those places. They were filled with false truces and all sorts of front-stabbing. I was good at workplace pirouette, staying up on my toes, hopping on fractured ankles. But taking the high road was usually the longest drop off the cliff. I tolerated that sort of thing because I had the pure intention of changing things from the inside. Looking back, I'm not sure I would do it again. My toes have been through enough.

So any place I enter, I have to ask: *Do I stay to change things from the inside? Or do I leave because no one will respect my needs?*

You might be good at changing a place. Sometimes you find out that they were waiting for somebody like you. But no one should *have* to stay in a harmful place to change it. Some of us can. Some of us were never meant to.

It might happen though. At some point or another, you'll be called to stay, to make waves.

There will be a time you'll need to speak up when everyone else is telling you to keep it down. You'll be doing the work of Paul's right-hand man Timothy, preaching *out of season*, when it isn't popular, when nobody seems to care. The time is coming when it will seem everyone and everything is working against you, *but you know this is where you're meant to stay*. You bring all of you, but more importantly, you trust the real Non-Negotiable, the divine constancy, a value over your life not based on outcome but born of grace.

Have you been there? I've visited that town, now and then. Those are some of the craziest seasons of growth I've ever had. Maybe it was from the sheer effort of perseverance, or it was from the exhilaration of being the only one speaking up. But for moments at a time, the person I am and the person that I *wanted to be* have come together. There was a razor-sharp focus, a resoluteness in the bones, a steady march against the wind. I was awake. I was sure. Even to a place that didn't care for what I brought, I still brought myself along.

I suppose that's what they mean when they say, *Own your voice.* You are fully yourself, even when nobody hears you right then.

CINDERELLA SERVANT

You need to know, sometimes you'll only be a link in the chain. One rung of the ladder. You're going to be a Cinderella in somebody's life, one spin around, one little stitch in the tapestry.

I was called to a Code Blue for a patient named Gerard on an overnight shift. I sat with the family. I felt like I was doing nothing; I sat there with them at three in the morning in their room, occasionally asking if they needed anything, for about an hour and a half. I was a non-offensive bump on a log.

The next week, Gerard's family sent me a beautiful handcrafted gift basket with a card. The card said the simple words, *You being there meant everything.*

They even spelled my name correctly. And in the basket, there were a dozen bags of peanuts. I'm allergic to peanuts. I laughed. I did something that I thought was nothing but meant everything—

and I got back peanuts. I thought about God's sense of humor, and maybe there was an ironic lesson in a gift that I was allergic to, and how sitting with someone at three a.m. can mean more than I could bear to understand.

Like my friend used to tell me, "You do your part, and sometimes the part that God does is none of your business."

You won't always see the fruit of the seed you planted. And a lot of times, the fruit isn't about making a difference. It's been you all along.

CHAPTER 12

Giving a Voice: I Got a Story to Tell

Empathy, Compassion, and Presence

If somebody at least listens, it's not too bad.
— J. D. SALINGER, *THE CATCHER IN THE RYE*[1]

LIGHTS OUT, SHADOWTOWN

I was working one of my last shifts of the residency, when suddenly I fell over. Lights out, Shadowtown. I came to and my stomach was swirling, my vision a milky collapsing vignette. Somebody moved the walls about twenty feet apart and spun them like a roulette wheel. I was on the floor and I tried to grab the room, and with both hands I managed to catch the floor again. I lugged myself over to a hallway to get to the ER.

This was the longest walk of my life. I woke up twice on the opposite wall, only two steps further than when I was last conscious.

Normally the halls were busy at the hospital, but I didn't see a single person. Maybe they had taken a look at my green skin and ran.

I got to the ER shaking and I didn't know which way was up. One of the nurses I worked with, Candace, fast-tracked me into a room. She held up my elbow for balance. I was ordered to strip down into a hospital gown. I got my vitals taken and blood drawn. I gave a urine sample. I got an X-ray and CT scan. I was rolled back to the room; my coworkers tried not to stare.

I went from visiting patients earlier in the day to being horizontal and helpless. Only two hours had passed when I began to feel lonely. The slightest movement of my wrist set off the IV alarm for a possible occlusion. I buzzed for the nurse to use the toilet, but I felt pretty bad about it; she had to disconnect everything and there was a perfectly good bedpan that she kept looking at the whole time. Every time a doctor passed by my door, I thought maybe *this* one was the doctor with my test results. They would glance at me and moonwalk out of there. My wife was still a long way out. My room had no windows. It was cold, sterile, flat.

Very quickly, I was losing my autonomy. I did the only thing I knew to do: I called for a chaplain.

One of the supervisors, Shayla, showed up.

"How are you?" she asked. I let loose. I must have started back in childhood, at two years old, to my first conceivable memory, all the way to debating over the bedpan.

No kidding, only weeks before I had passed out in the hallway, I had been in a car accident; my car was totaled. Someone had hit me with identity theft and tried to take over 40,000 dollars out of my account (I have never had that much money at once, ever). I was still getting over my dad's life-threatening illness.

Shayla listened. She didn't look away once. She asked if she could pray for me. Of course, I said. And she prayed. She put words around all the things I was thinking and feeling; she said all the words I couldn't say. I tried not to weep, but I did anyway.

In her prayer, at the very end, she said:

Thank You, God, for seeing us. For hearing us.

That meant a lot to me. To be seen and to be heard.

I think it means everything.

— — —

I turned out okay, by the way. "Low blood sugar and low blood pressure is all," the doctor said. "Eat a granola bar and stand up slowly, like you're under a tripwire." She giggled a lot at this idea. It did get my blood pressure back up.

The next day, I realized something. Shayla had shown up to my bedside wearing plain clothes. She hadn't been working when I fell over. She had just shown up.

LOOK HERE, TAKE A LISTEN

The goal of chaplaincy, one of the supervisors said, is that *we listen to the patient as if they are the only person in the world.*

The temptation, we were told, is that when somebody shares a story, we go into *advice-giving.* I mean, giving advice is meant to help. But it's a one-way megaphone. It doesn't give life or hope or a chance. And it cuts a story short.

We learned that "un-listened" stories are an open wound,

always sore, demanding care. Many of us carry those around. If someone *does* get a chance to share their story and someone listens, I mean really *listens*, usually they find catharsis. Closure. An exhalation. I don't mean that things change, but the thing itself is made real and respected, and there's the possibility of a new strength to get through the unresolved. Like psychologist Carl Rogers says, "When I have been listened to and when I have been heard, I am able to re-perceive my world in a new way and to go on. It is astonishing how elements that seem insoluble become soluble when someone listens, how confusions that seem irremediable turn into relatively clear flowing streams when one is heard."[2]

The hard thing is that most people never get to tell their stories. Mostly because it's hard to listen, and some of us—many of us, including me—can be pretty bad at listening.

— — —

I was called to this patient who was being "difficult." When I got to her room, she had her arms crossed and a look that could bruise somebody. I introduced myself and she said "harumph" and turned away from me. No kidding. I tried again and she did the same thing—*harumph*—and she turned farther. I went to the other side of the bed because I couldn't see her face, and can you believe it, she *harumph*'ed and turned her head back toward the door I had entered.

I remembered our training: *underneath the story that people tell is the one they're really living.*

The patient's answers were short and sharp. "Surgery. Yeah. That's all. No. I'm fine."

I decided to leave and I asked, "Is there something I can get for you before your surgery?"—and she burst into tears.

"I want it back!" she yelled. She slammed both her fists into the bed and bounced up and down. A real tantrum.

"What did you want back?" I asked.

She said, "They took my stuff. They keep your stuff during surgery. My notebook was in there and I have to journal when I'm stressed. They told me the surgery was in ten minutes, and it's been an hour. I need my notebook."

That was it. I made a call to get her notebook. I waited with her.

We ended up talking for an hour. She told me she was on her fifth surgery. The other four had failed. She was divorced; she lived alone; she hadn't had any success with dating; she said it was due to her condition. The surgery, she thought, was her one shot to be herself again.

She did get her notebook. By the time it came, she was feeling mostly okay.

I had to wonder if it was really the notebook she needed or just for someone to know it was important to her. Or both.

IT'S REAL, I TELL YOU

There's a classic dispute among psychologists that's best shown by the hair dryer story.[3]

It goes like this: A woman gets obsessed with the idea that her hair dryer is going to burn down her house. She gets to work, but she keeps driving back to her house to make sure it's still intact. It gets to be a real problem; she's driving back home ten, twenty times a day. Her work life and love life and social life all take a hit. She tries therapy and medication, but neither help. Finally, she sees a therapist. He asks her, "Say, have you thought about just bringing the hair dryer with you?"

It works. When the fear creeps in, the woman opens her drawer in her office and looks at the hair dryer and she's fine.

Some psychologists see a major problem with this, that it's somehow enabling delusions or fantasies. *Nothing was solved! She still has issues! She needs to get to the root of it!* But others might say she found a solution that worked *for her*. I lean toward the second camp. The problem was real to her and so was the solution. Maybe later, some advice might reach her and she would get to the bottom of her thing. But until then, she had found a way to make it okay.

The big idea is that her story was taken seriously. That was the start of her wholeness. And only when a story is fully heard is there the possibility of connection or challenge or growth.

SECRET ASIAN MAN

This idea of *giving a voice* is very important to me. It's important because by default, hardly anybody gives me the time of day. About a dozen times a week, I'm reminded that I'm not as "real" as other people.

Here's what I mean. I was getting out of my car once in the parking lot and somebody next to me opened their door on my leg. He took a look at me, turned to his friend, and whispered, "It's just a Chinese guy." You know, a billion more where we came from.

One of the things about being an Asian-American is that I'm hardly heard. I don't have much of a voice at all. The first time I heard the song "Secret Agent Man," I thought the singer was saying *Secret Asian Man*. I thought it was about being unseen. It's true though. The second I see an Asian-American on screen, they get wrapped up in a punchline or a plot device. They don't have their own hopes and fears; they serve either as exotic decoration or the enemy element which must be erased. Once in a while, someone will explain things to me very slowly, as if I'm a clueless, wide-eyed foreigner. In my first American history class in college, we got to *Asian-Americans* and the professor declared, "We're skipping this. It's a small chunk, anyway." Right over the China Exclusion Act, Japanese internment camps, Chinese slaves who built the Central Pacific Railroad, and the Korean War, *also known as the Forgotten War*. Everyone in class turned to look at me in the back. I said nothing. I remained silent in the back, in my place.

The message I usually get is, *Be grateful, you're smart, you have it easy*. Or, *You people are the most privileged*. Maybe that's true. All I know is that I've been second-class and picked last as long as I can remember. You won't see many of us protesting or taking a knee, usually because we're passive but mostly because it doesn't do much. I'm the kind of guy you can yell at in traffic without feeling bad; I've seen a special kind of rage at stoplights, always with the undertone, *I should've known it was you people*.

I try not to talk about this much because it sounds like I'm whining. I try to "raise my voice" on social media and it becomes a ghost town, tumbleweeds and shuffling feet. I get that. It's an icky topic. I wish I could express how lonely it is without making you feel weird about it. But it's all the lonelier when nobody cares you're lonely.

I was talking about this issue with a fellow chaplain, and after I told her three or four stories of being invisible, she nearly burst into tears. She hadn't realized how hard it was for a guy like me to enter a room as equals. She shared with me what it was like to be a woman and the sort of mistreatment she gets at a gas station or grocery store or even her church. We found a lot of common ground. The main thing is, she heard me and I heard her. That didn't fix everything, no. But for that day, at least, I was almost a person. Someone recognized that I had real thoughts and anxieties. *We spoke the same language and shared a voice.* That's rare for me. It's as rare as finding somebody who listens.

"There is no agony like bearing an untold story inside you," Zora Neale Hurston said.[4] So there must be no greater relief than to speak that story.

WHEN THERE ARE NO WORDS

I spoke with Red Hong Yi, a renowned artist in Malaysia, who also wrote the foreword to this book. Her whole thing is that she paints without brushes. Her most famous pieces are a portrait of Jackie Chan using chopsticks and a shadow art of *Star Wars* characters using various things like flowers, feathers, twigs, and leaves. Her videos have millions of views online. But I think the best thing about her is her heart for charity, for places like Syria and Lebanon and Nepal.

Red often uses her art to bring awareness to a lot of social issues. Her art also brings happiness to a lot of people affected by those issues. But I think one of the coolest things I heard is when Red went to a school with Syrian refugee children and taught them how to use art as a creative outlet, with objects like chopsticks, forks, spoons, socks, and basketballs.

The refugees needed this. Across the border, right over the hills past the school, there was an ongoing war back home. Many of the refugees still kept the keys to their houses in Syria. The houses were probably gone, but they kept the keys as mementos. You could say that Red, if anything, helped the refugees to unlock their memories.

The chaplains did a similar thing in the hospital: we'd bring a coloring book and construction paper and markers to a patient. Some of the patients who didn't like to talk out loud would talk through their drawings, or they'd tell their story while coloring, or they'd finally feel relaxed with a marker in their hands, creating something. This seems like a simple idea. But it's a really big deal. Art has the power to give a different kind of voice to people. And the bigger point is this: *Not everybody needs somebody to speak for them, but they instead need the right tools to speak on their own.*

Red gave the refugees a medium with which to express themselves. That was the breakthrough. She wasn't trying to speak for them. She was giving them a way to speak for themselves.

A WORD FOR YOU:

Now Hear Me Out

You're going to have a voice when somebody won't. And somebody is going to need a voice. It matters then what you do.

It's a good idea to speak up for that person, sure. But even better, I hope that you can *pass the microphone*. The paintbrush. The podium. To those who never had one. For the marginalized, those pushed to the sidelines. That's what real empathy is. Not just entering, but empowering.

So we ask: *What do they need most? What works for them and their community? What would actually help? What would definitely not help? What do I have wrong about them? How can I listen to their story on their terms?*

— — —

I'm sure you've been in the pain of a situation where nobody heard you. Nobody believed you. Or you got a lot of advice thrown your way. Whether it was your mental health or grief or a chronic illness or about being a minority, nobody listened.

Here are a few things you need to know.

One is that you might be lonely for a while. I know that's no fun to hear, but that's the hard truth of it. For me, saying that out loud—*I'm lonely*—gave me some relief that I wasn't going crazy.

Two is that some of your friends *do* want to hear you, but

they're not sure how. They don't know the right words or context or history. They'll stumble around a bit. They'll need your help. It shouldn't be on you to educate them, but they're willing to learn from you.

Three is that there are always people who will listen. Your issue, no matter how oddly specific, has a community. I believe it. I don't believe that God is going to leave us alone on that. It might take a while to find them, but there's a group of people out there who have been in your valley, clawed at its crevices, crawled through its shadows. That doesn't make them perfect or even polite. But it means they're around. It just takes the one.

YOUR PAIN IS MY PAIN

I was that one, once.

I'm twenty-one-years-old and I've swallowed half a bottle of acetaminophen. At the hospital, my brother is there. "That must've been some headache," he says, and we laugh. In the middle of laughing, I throw up everywhere. The nurse had given me a cup of charcoal to neutralize the acid in my stomach. My vomit is the color of midnight. My body is ejecting a nightmare.

One of the nurses tells me, "You've been Baker Act'ed." Like it was a gameshow. It's a seventy-two hour hold. I get moved from the hospital to a mental institution called Bay Care or Bay Pointe or Bay Life. It might as well be Bay Prison. By the end of three days, I lose thirteen pounds and one of my socks.

The patients and I go to this group meeting, and the lead counselor passes out these giant rubber pens and circular sheets of paper. He asks us, "What's your goal today?" One of the guys pulls the fire alarm and yells that he'll never stop doing favors for crack. "It's a free country," he yells, while two nurses sedate him and drag him across the linoleum. He's still yelling but the fire alarm drowns him out. The counselor asks again, "What's your goal today?" I write down, *To get out.*

That night, my bunkmate wakes me up. He's the same guy they dragged out of the meeting. He's spinning his mattress over his head and he tells me, "Roaches in my bed, my veins, come on, it's true, it's really true!"

I watch him for a minute. I know my options. I can grab a counselor to stop him. I can ask to switch rooms. I can tell the guy, "It's not true, you're hallucinating, that's why you're here."

"Hey," I tell him. "I know. Let's look for them, you know? If we don't find any, we can sleep, how's that? Let's look for them together."

My bunkmate likes this plan. We get on our hands and knees to look for cockroaches. After thirty seconds, he gets back on his mattress and falls asleep.

— — —

I've told this story before and it makes me sound like a hero. But honestly, I was just tired. I wanted to sleep for a thousand years. I thought the easiest thing to do would be to enter my bunkmate's delusion and humor him. By accident, I touched upon something that has since informed the way I treat people. The way I treat their mental health. The way I treat their feelings of loneliness, of being unheard, of being a minority, of being silenced.

If it's important to you, it's important to me. If it's real to you, it's real to me. If it hurts you, it hurts me. Your pain is my pain.

I think about my old bunkmate sometimes. Can you imagine believing that you have bugs in your veins? I still think of the look in his eyes, the way he tore at the inside of his forearms. Never mind that what he felt wasn't true. It was true for him. If you say your problem is true, I want to meet you there.

Is that dangerous? It could be. And some situations are way over my head. But in this very moment, I want to hear you. With my very limited ability, I want to understand. Then, and only then, can we get somewhere.

— — —

On one of my last visits of the chaplaincy program, I visited a patient, Kyrone, who was homeless. He had a lot of issues, the main one being that he was dying.

He was a young guy, body misshapen at every joint and trying his best to smile. He told me, "They think my kind is tougher. Like we can just take it. Sleeping under bridges, eating from dumpsters. You can't imagine it, right? I didn't get any tougher. I feel all of it, like anybody would. I can't bear it, chap."

Kyrone saw my face. He said, "Chap, I'm sorry. Don't cry, brother. You know why I'm smiling? Because I sing. I write songs."

I asked him if I could hear one.

And Kyrone sang. He sang about a home he never had and wanting to go there. He sang about children being as tall as adults so they wouldn't have to be under anyone. He sang a wish that his disease could be healed by kind words, just as his soul had been. He sang, *You are seen, I am seen, and so we are heard.*

I was Kyrone's audience, the hospital bed his stage, and Kyrone was the most important person in the world. His voice was quiet but it filled the room, and for a moment it seemed his disfigured body had regained shape. I understood right then the righteous power of silence, never to be used over someone, but always *for*, and that every person has a song they must sing—a song that will not be silenced.

I wept, and I'm sure it was unprofessional, but I refused to hold back the ocean of all that was inside. This was my favorite and hardest part of being a chaplain, you know. Weeping with. Sharing pain. Becoming the other. It's hard to, and I'm glad to.

After Kyrone finished, he told me, "Nobody heard these before. They will one day, won't they?"

"They will." I wiped my tears and told him, "You're famous to me, Kyrone."

Kyrone died an hour after our visit. I was called back up, and I wept over his broken body. *I'm sorry,* I told him. *I'm sorry that no one else got to hear your songs.* I said that for a long time, until a nurse came to check on me. It was hard to pull away. It's such a terrible thing when a voice goes unheard. I have seen so many voices die, and I pray to God it is enough that I have heard them one more time.

When the nurses cleaned Kyrone, his body seemed to be restful, comfortable. Not bent at all angles like before. It had to be a trick of the light, I thought. But I have learned, in all my time with all my patients, that each one holds a story that must be given voice, and very often it's only in their telling that there is healing—or that healing comes by song. If we are made for God and for each other, then our separation is a wound, and when we hear each other, I believe that His grace enters there and mends us together.

> *The stories people tell have a way of taking care of them.*
> —BARRY LOPEZ, *CROW AND WEASEL*[5]

"It's weird, what we do," Rebecca told me. "Like what did I even do all day? How do I explain what a chaplain does?"

I shrugged. "It *is* weird. We just . . . sit there. And something happens."

I think it was said best by Kerry Egan, a hospice chaplain: "All I can do is show up and listen. This, as strange as it sounds, is where a chaplain's power lies, in the powerlessness of the role."[6]

To give up power, that others may have some, has honestly been the greatest experience of my life. I can think of no higher honor, no better calling, and nothing I am more thankful for than my patients, who let me hear their voices, and so often their last breath. I will carry them always.

I AM SPOKEN FOR

You need to know that I've failed at this. I've failed at speaking up for people. Failed at hearing them. A whole lot. And many have failed to hear me a whole lot too. I've been silent or silenced.

I think about the moment when Pontius Pilate, the Roman governor of Judea, pushes both Jesus and a criminal named

Barabbas onto a public courtyard. Pilate asks which man should be set free. You know what's coming. The crowd, in unison, yells, *Barabbas.* They choose the criminal.[7]

Christ was then led to His cross like a lamb to His shearers. Silent. Silenced. Deserted. Torn to shreds. He was sentenced at night, illegally, so nobody could intervene. With the kiss of His disciple Judas still fresh on His cheek and with the denial of Peter still ringing in His ears, Jesus was cast to the edge of the city, Golgotha, the site of the skull. He was hung on a cross. The sun darkened over Him. His mouth was sealed by a cursed sponge. His body was sealed in an airtight corner, unmarked and unremarkable.

This tells me at least two things. One is that *He knows what it's like to be silenced.* To have no one speak up for Him. In a way, you could say He was silenced *with* us. Christ, in His humanness, was voiceless, like you and I are sometimes. Two is that He was silenced *for* us. Jesus could've ripped open the sky with His fingertips. But He didn't retaliate. Instead, He absorbed the cosmic violence of being unheard. And when He did speak, He said, "Father, forgive them, for they do not know what they are doing."[8] All the power in the galaxy, and He used it to speak grace.

This is how He used His voice. To advocate for us still. That's a wild truth, considering that when I see the cross, it might as well have been me up there. I'm sure that I have been Barabbas. I have been Peter. I have been Judas. Or one of the bloodthirsty crowd. I have used my voice for unspeakable things. But Christ hung there with His voice cut off, so we could have a voice. His cross was solidarity. His cross was advocacy. And so too, His cross was a picture of all the times I failed to speak. But so He went on that wretched tree, to set a person like me free.

Here's what I know. The gospel story tells me there is a divine voice, a perfect melody of love and justice. That voice forgives me for all the times that I didn't speak up. That voice compels me to speak when I least want to. And that voice says I am heard.

Because I am heard, I can speak.

In the surplus of that divine worth, I am moved to hear others and to speak up for those whose voices were stolen. For me, that's love. That's justice. Christ does the same for you too. He hears you when no one else does. He gives you a voice when no one else will.

That's the story I believe about the world, as best as I can tell it. For me, that's the pulse of the universe. I hear a voice from an empty tomb that calls for Peter, despite him.[9] Christ calls my name and yours. He speaks life, so that we'd do the same.

You are loved much to love much.

You are spoken for, to speak.

One Voice

THE POWER OF UNITY

This is the final thing I learned.

I can either become a voice that someone has to overcome, or a voice that helps someone to overcome.

A year after the chaplaincy program, I was on a shift and one of the chaplains handed me a note.

"From a patient's daughter," he said. I must have made a face, so he added, "It's not bad. Or weird. You'll see."

I opened the note:

> A year and a half ago, you were my chaplain. You were there when my father died. You didn't say much, but you sat with me and it meant a lot. Honestly, I had planned on ending it all that day. But you prayed a prayer about my dad's life living through me. I'm still here because of what you said. I never forgot it.

I've thought about the many people that I could write this same note to. The people who sat with me. Who said the right thing at the right time. Who probably couldn't remember how they breathed life through me right then. I remember Benjamin, who didn't mind being friends with me in my junior year of high school when no one would be, and I remember Travis in sixth grade, who kept me safe from the bigger kids who kept trying to steal my glasses.

I've thought about how many people might be all right if they got a note with some kind of encouragement.

I think about Victor, the kid in sixth grade whose face was undone, and how maybe he could've gone another way instead of dropping out of everything. I think about Jonathan, who was addicted to heroin and telling fake stories about wrestling championships, who eventually overdosed one summer before his thirtieth birthday. I think about Nolan, a guy that I met in church who wanted to become gym buddies with me or at least get a coffee, and a month later he ingested a bottle of pills and died in his sleep. I wonder if just the one time at the gym or an espresso would've sent his life in another direction.

I wonder if I could've helped them. I think about how so many had helped me.

I've thought about the many people that I would never write a nice note to. They stick harder in my memory sometimes. A guy named Todd who was my math tutor, who yelled at me at the top of his lungs, who made me write math formulas a thousand times (which never got me better at math) and who lied to my parents about my progress—I've never forgotten him, and I have mixed anger and embarrassment every time I remember his fingers digging into my shoulders. I remember bullies like Will and Christopher and Melvin and Dillon, who fancied themselves twice as big because they beat up guys half their size. I remember a guy named Denny, a student at my dad's dojo, who grabbed my brother inappropriately, and how we were too young to understand what was happening.

I'd like to think that all of them were the way they were because they never heard the gracious words that they needed. I guess they never got a nice note.

In sixth grade on the last day of the school year, the two girls who had given me an *Ugly Pass,* Briana and Sheena, came up to me and apologized. They were sobbing and everything, and I think they meant it. I opened my arms for a hug but they ran away from the awkwardness of the moment, and I understood that we were just twelve years old trying to figure out the power of our words and that words can really mean something. They can make a floppy sixth grader feel a little less lonely and almost help him believe that his entire school year wasn't a terrible sentence on the rest of his life.

I remember when I was a youth pastor, I had this breakdown about ten minutes before I had to give the sermon to a bunch of students, so I called my mom and told her that I was done. I couldn't do it anymore. I couldn't face one more disinterested, distracted high schooler. *I quit,* I kept saying. I was in the back room behind the pulpit and there was a window behind me: *I could sneak out easy, Mom, I could jump from the second floor to the nearest bush and hide until they call the police.* I don't remember everything that my mom said. I only remember her saying, *You are a good pastor. You are a good son.* I wiped my eyes and I gave the worst, weirdest sermon of my life—but I had my mom's words ringing in my ear and I was floating on air the whole time.

I remember entering the conference room for my final evalua-

267

tion in the chaplaincy program, and there were Audrey and Frida and Shayla and Rebecca and all the chaplains who were going to grill me, and they all stood in unison and bowed. Like a real, respectful bow, way past ninety degrees.

"How did you feel about that?" Audrey asked.

"You are my superiors," I said. "So naturally my stomach did a thing."

"What sort of thing did your stomach do?"

"A back-flip. And then—it unclenched. Do you have to write down 'unclenched'?"

"What would be a better word?"

"I think *safe.* I felt safe. Like you hear me. Like I have a voice here."

— — —

We carry voices, but they can carry us too. They can keep us locked up, or they can keep us safe, or they can make us sick, or they can make us well, or they can poke us full of holes or they can, you know, make us whole.

They can divide us. They can bring us close.

I'm at this hospital bed where a one-hundred-year-old woman is breathing her last breath, and her entire family of daughters and sons is singing "Amazing Grace." They sound like angels. Only an hour earlier, they had been fighting about their mother's house and which sister hadn't visited enough and who was going to call the funeral home, but at least for now, they were singing over their mother in a single voice. On both sides of me, the patient's son and daughter grab my hand and the son nods at me, as if to say, *Be yourself with us,* and that's his invitation for me to sing.

I wish I could tell you that I was brave enough to join their singing that day. I only moved my lips. I only stood in their circle. I hoped it was enough. Maybe it was. But I wish I would've sung.

There are a thousand notes I have not written and a thousand notes I have not sung—but the invitation has always been open, to give the best of me that I can give, to sing along, to be myself.

~ ~ ~

I was on the Mindoro Island of the Philippines. I was in a tiny hut that they called a church. It was the only building on the entire island that had electricity and a concrete floor. The pastor's wife played a busted guitar with five strings. A group of about fifty people from the island huddled close and sang a song in their native tongue, Tagalog. Everybody sang loud and danced around, enough to make the light bulbs sway. Nobody was singing on key because they were half-laughing and half-crying, as loud as I had ever heard, and their dancing made the church a living, pulsing, thriving organism.

I didn't know the words to the songs. But I sang along, curving my mouth the best I could, trying to get the lyrics just right. I was the only guy trying to sound like I knew what I was doing.

Be yourself with us, I thought.

And at some point, I quit trying to sound like a professional. I dropped the vocal modulations. I let my voice do what it wanted to do. Soon I didn't care who was listening or looking. I sang as bad and as loud as I wanted to. I kicked off my shoes and danced on sacred ground.

I don't think I have much of a voice—but what I do have is mine, after all.

When I looked around, I thought about that verse in Scripture—*a great multitude that no one could count, from every nation, tribe, people and language*[1]—and I heard the Mindoro people's individual voices like the texture of rain across an ocean, and I heard their voices in unison too, the rush of warm water over bruised hands. I think I was crying with them, and laughing, but whatever I was doing, I was singing. My singing was bad. It was horrendous. It was wonderful. My voice was their voice and their voice was mine. For that moment we were bonded by the Spirit that made us, the Spirit that wants to breathe in you too.

I thought of another verse, *No one has ever seen God; but if we love one another, God lives in us and his love is made complete in us.*[2] I know God was breathing His love into our lungs then. A love like that can make a hut into a palace, and our singing into the voices of angels. On that island, in that hut, with all the love we had in that room, we were so many, and we were one.

I hope you know you are seen and heard and loved by that same Spirit.

I hope you choose to be carried by that divine voice, the one who sings over you.

I hope you know that you're brave enough to join the song.

You are.

You really are.

I developed the Internal Voices model as early as 2012, but like any model, it was inspired and informed by many sources, such as:

Karen Horney's views on mental health from her works *Neurosis and Human Growth: The Struggle Toward Self-Realization* (1950) and *The Neurotic Personality of Our Time* (1937)

Alice Miller's model of grandiosity and depression from *The Drama of the Gifted Child* (1979)

The work of Brené Brown, in particular *Daring Greatly* (2012)

Various concepts espoused by C. S. Lewis, in particular from *Mere Christianity* (1952) and *God in the Dock* (1970)

Timothy Keller's take on the gospel from his sermon "Spiritual Warfare" (Jan. 2012) and "The Gospel" (Jan. 2005)

Edward H. Hagen's Bargaining Model of Anger and Depression, from two of his studies (2003, 2016)

Boundaries (1992, 2017) by Henry Cloud and John Townsend

I developed the "Main Character Syndrome" as early as 2013. Similar ideas have been floating around for a while, such as the Karpman Triangle, themes of imperialism, the philosophical theory of solipsism, and the much-lambasted hero-savior narrative.

For my External Voices model, I was inspired by my chaplaincy program. The trauma portion was informed by the ACE Study, first developed by Vincent Felitti in a study of over 17,000 participants (1998). My take on guilt was a personal battle I had throughout the entire program, in the end remedied by conversations with my supervisors and, to my surprise, the research on trauma. For family dynamics, I adapted this partially from the Family Systems Theory of Murray Bowen, who developed the Eight Concepts model (about 1960s), and I combined it with some eastern sensibilities. My take on grief was informed anecdotally by the over one thousand patients I've visited, and was partially informed by Atul Gawande's work *Being Mortal* (2014).

I first shared the Voices model in the summer of 2012 with my youth group. At the time, I was working with Asian-American youth students who swung wildly between extremes of self-doubt and pride. Observing my wonderful students (and my own pastoral performance) is what first gave rise to the Voices model.

The title of my book is inspired by *The Things They Carried* (1990) by Tim O'Brien.

And to reiterate what is stated on the copyright page: the names and details of some stories have been changed to protect the privacy of individuals.

J. S. Park

Acknowledgments

There are too many people to thank. I'm going to miss someone, but I promise I didn't mean to.

Thank you: My wife, Juliette. My brother, Hoon. To my parents, my in-laws, my sibling-in-laws, my cousins, my dog Rosco. Where would I be without you? Looking out a window in the corner, most likely.

My coworkers: Each of you, in some way, whether large or small, have seen me and heard me. I sit in your shadows, rooting for you, grateful to be your support, sidekick, and cheerleader in your stories. I want to name every single one of you, but I've been notified that the Acknowledgments must be contained to these two pages. Thank you to Waleska, Jenny, Alisha, and Laura for allowing me to include you in this story.

Thank you to the incredible team at Moody Publishers. Amy and Amanda are the best editors in the world. Thank you to Siri, Ashley, Randall, Erik, Grace, Mackenzie, Connor, Josh, Rachel, Brock, Richard, Pamela, Judy, Kate and the many others I met when I visited your headquarters. Thank you to DJ, my amazing agent, and the entire team at Legacy for your confidence in me.

Thank you to the many pastors and their families who have been a blessing: Pastor Paul and Deborah, P. Jae and Esther, P. Mike, P. Pedro, P. Jake, P. Steve, Peter M., P. Erik and Sarah, P. Jeff K., P. Danny, P. Baik, P. Calvin and Jeanette, and many others I'm missing.

Thank you: Austin, Andre, Jacob, Rev. Beth, Beth O., and many others for letting me go on and on about the book. To Amanda Jones and Hannah Gregory for reading early drafts. To Rob and T.B. for being early supporters. To the many therapists I've had and those in the mental health field: stay encouraged, you are what we need.

Thank you: Red Hong Yi, Pastor Eugene Cho, Josh Riebock, Yumi, Jae Jin, Danah and Stacey, and Craig Gross for allowing me to interview each of you. You inspire me. Thank you to Heather Parady, Justin Khoe, and Sam Won for finding me interesting enough to interview. Thank you to Kyle and Michelle R., who connected me with Jordan Raynor, who connected me with his agent.

To the many people who I've met online, who messaged me motivation and cheered me on and stayed with me on this journey: You make this world better. Thank you. I see you. I hear you.

Thank you to my patients. I changed so many details to keep you secret, but your voices are alive at the edges. I am but a footnote; you are the champions of your stories.

To John E: I'm sorry. We were supposed to get Korean BBQ. We were supposed to go to the gym together, or lift bricks outdoors on your patio. I never got to tell you I was writing a book. I hope I have honored you.

Thank you, God. To Jesus: Where would I be without you? Looking out a window in the corner, not wearing pants even. But truly, you entered, and nothing tasted the same again. You gave me pants, and colors, and filled my pockets with so much soul I can hardly stand it.

Notes

INTRODUCTION

1. Frederick Buechner, *The Sacred Journey: A Memoir of Early Days* (New York: HarperCollins, 1982), 6. Formatting mine.
2. Julian Leff, Geoffrey Williams, Mark A. Huckvale, Maurice Arbuthnot, and Alex P. Leff, "Computer-assisted therapy for medication-resistant auditory hallucinations: proof-of-concept study," *The British Journal of Psychiatry* 202, no. 6 (June 2013): 428–33.
3. Tom KJ Craig, Mar Rus-Calafell, Thomas Ward, Julian P. Leff, Mark Huckvale, Elizabeth Howarth, Richard Emsley, Philippa A. Garety, "AVATAR therapy for auditory verbal hallucinations in people with psychosis: a single-blind, randomised controlled trial," *Lancet Psychiatry* 5, no. 1 (January 2018): 31–40.

CHAPTER 1

1. Tim O'Brien, *The Things They Carried* (New York: Houghton Mifflin, 1990, 2009), 9.

CHAPTER 2

1. Raymond Chandler, *The Big Sleep* (New York: Vintage Books, 1939, 1992), 70.
2. C. S. Lewis, *God in the Dock: Essays on Theology and Ethics* (Grand Rapids, MI: Eerdmans, 1970, 2014), 163.
3. Psychologist Jonathan Haidt says this is our "in-house press secretary," which gives post hoc reasoning to support our past actions and advance our agenda. Jonathan Haidt, *The Righteous Mind* (New York: Vintage Books, 2012, 2013), 91–92.
4. Carol Tavris and Elliot Aronson, *Mistakes Were Made (But Not by Me): Why We Justify Foolish Beliefs, Bad Decisions, and Hurtful Acts* (New York: Houghton Mifflin Court, 2007, 2015), 5.
5. Raymond Chandler, *The Little Sister* (New York: Vintage, 1949, 1988), 13.
6. Joseph Luft and Harrington Ingham, "The Johari window, a graphic model of interpersonal awareness," *Proceedings of the Western Training Laboratory in Group Development* (Los Angeles: UCLA, Extension Office, 1955). Joseph Luft, *Group Processes: An Introduction to Group Dynamics* (Palo Alto, CA: Mayfield Publishing Company, 1963, 1970), 60.
7. Emily Dickinson, *Emily Dickinson: Selected Poems* (1890; repr., London: Phoenix, 2003), 81.
8. Justin Kruger and David Dunning, "Unskilled and Unaware of It: How Difficulties in Recognizing One's Own Incompetence Lead to Inflated Self-Assessments," *Journal of Personality and Social Psychology* 77, no. 6 (December 1999): 1121–34a. The study has been reassessed several times. It's been noted that in certain cultures, such as the East, there's a tendency to underestimate one's own skill level.
9. Ryan Holiday, *Ego Is the Enemy* (New York: Portfolio, 2017), 2, 4.
10. The concept of the Einstellung effect was first developed and tested by psychologist Abraham Luchins in 1942. Jessica Ellis and Eyal Reingold, "The Einstellung effect in anagram

problem solving: evidence from eye movements," *Frontiers in Psychology* 5, Art. 679 (July 2, 2014).

11. Brené Brown, *Daring Greatly: How the Courage to Be Vulnerable Transforms the Way We Live, Love, Parent, and Lead* (New York: Penguin, 2012, 2015), 21–22.

12. Harriet Lerner, *The Dance of Connection: How to Talk to Someone When You're Mad, Hurt, Scared, Frustrated, Insulted, Betrayed, or Desperate* (New York: HarperCollins, 2001, 2002), 197.

13. Dr. Tasha Eurich talks about this correlation in three places: her book *Insight: The Surprising Truth About How Others See Us, How We See Ourselves, and Why the Answers Matter More Than We Think,* particularly in chapters 3 and 4 (New York: Currency, 2017, 2018); a podcast interview on *Radio Times with Marty Moss-Coane* where she was also interviewed alongside Dr. David Dunning who coined the Dunning-Kruger Effect; and an online interview with *The Cut* on Oct. 3, 2017.

14. Tim O'Brien, *The Things They Carried* (New York: Houghton Mifflin, 1990, 2009), 82.

15. Kerry Patterson, Joseph Grenny, Ron McMillan, Al Switzler, *Crucial Conversations: Tools for Talking When Stakes Are High* (New York: McGraw-Hill, 2002, 2012), 55–56.

CHAPTER 3

1. Raymond Chandler, *Trouble Is My Business* (New York: Vintage Books, 1934, 1992), 130.

2. Haruki Murakami, *Blind Willow, Sleeping Woman* (New York: Vintage Books, 2006), 235.

3. Karen Horney's theories on personality, developed over her lifetime as a practicing psychoanalyst, were later tested in a personality survey of 1,079 total participants in 2001. Surveys were done again with various sample sizes in 2004, 2011, 2014, and 2015. Karen Horney's theories were found to be highly reliable descriptors and predictors not only for "neurotics," but personality types in general.
   Frederick L. Coolidge, Candace J. Moor, Tomoko G. Yamazaki, Sharon E. Stewart, Daniel L. Segal, "On the relationship between Karen Horney's tripartite neurotic type theory and personality disorder features," *Personality and Individual Difference 30*, no. 8 (June 2001): 1387–1400.

4. Karen Horney, *Neurosis and Human Growth* (New York: Norton & Company, 1950), 18–19.

5. Ibid., 13.

6. Ibid., 111. Emphasis mine.

7. Thomas Curran, Andrew P. Hill, "Perfectionism Is Increasing Over Time: A Meta-Analysis of Birth Cohort Differences From 1989 to 2016," *Psychological Bulletin* 145, no. 4 (December 2017): 410–429.
   Excerpt: "We speculate [perfectionism has increased over the last 27 years] because, generally, American, Canadian, and British cultures have become more individualistic, materialistic, and socially antagonistic over this period, with young people now facing more competitive environments, more unrealistic expectations, and more anxious and controlling parents than generations before."

8. Liu yi Lin, Jaime E. Sidani, Ariel Shensa, Ana Radovic, Elizabeth Miller, Jason B. Colditz, Beth L. Hoffman, Leila M. Giles, and Brian A. Primack, "Association between Social Media Use and Depression among U.S. Young Adults," *Depression and Anxiety.* 33, no. 4 *April 2016): 323–31. This study suggests that those already with underlying depression might find comfort in social media. But the study also suggests that "exposure to highly idealized representations of peers on social media elicits feelings of envy and the

distorted belief that others lead happier and/or more successful lives. Consequently, these envious feelings may lead to a sense of self-inferiority and depression over time."

9. Charlene Y. Chen Nanyang, Maya Rossignac-Milon, and E. Tory Higgins, "Feeling Distressed From Making Decisions: Assessors' Need to Be Right," *Journal of Personality and Social Psychology* 115, no. 4 (February 2018): 743–61.

10. William Butler Yeats, *Responsibilities and Other Poems* (New York: The Macmillan Company, 1916).

11. It could also be depression. For that, and really in general, I will always recommend therapy, medicine, and every other resource for mental health available to you.

12. Karen Horney, *The Neurotic Personality of Our Time* (New York: Norton & Company, 1937), 51.

13. Increasing self-esteem is not a bad thing, but the methods themselves were discovered to be self-sabotaging and counter-productive.

   Roy F. Baumeister, Jennifer D. Campbell, Joachim I. Krueger, and Kathleen D. Vohs, "Does High Self-Esteem Cause Better Performance, Interpersonal Success, Happiness, or Healthier Lifestyles?," *Psychological Science in the Public Interest* 4, no. 1 (May 2003): 1–44.

14. Karen Horney, *Neurosis and Human Growth* (New York: Norton & Company, 1950), 111. Emphasis mine.

15. *Creed*, directed by Ryan Coogler, screenplay by Ryan Coogler and Aaron Covington (Burbank, CA: Warner Bros., 2015).

16. Joan C. Harvey and Cynthia Katz, "If I'm So Successful, Why Do I Feel like a Fake? The Impostor Phenomenon" (New York: St. Martin's Press, 1985), 3.

   John Gravois, "You're Not Fooling Anyone," *The Chronicle of Higher Education* 54, no. 11 (2007): 1.

   Pauline Rose Clance, who first coined Impostor Syndrome in 1978, has also developed a quiz: http://paulineroseclance.com/pdf/IPTestandscoring.pdf.

17. Personal interview with Eugene Cho, Quest Church, Seattle, WA, October 17, 2017.

18. Ibid.

19. Richard Gardner, Jeffrey Bednar, Bryan Stewart, James Oldroyd, Joseph Moore, "'I Must Have Slipped through the Cracks Somehow': An Examination of Coping with Perceived Impostorism and the Role of Social Support," *Journal of Vocational Behavior* 115 (December 2019).

20. *Star Trek: The Next Generation*, "Peak Performance," season 2, episode 21, directed by Robert Scheerer, written by David Kemper, aired July 10, 1989.

21. Tobias Tempel and Roland Neumann, "Taming Test Anxiety: The Activation of Failure-Related Concepts Enhances Cognitive Test Performance of Test-Anxious Students," *The Journal of Experimental Education* 84, no. 4 (February 2016): 702–22. See also the research of Kristalyn Salters-Pedneault, Matthew Tull, and Lizabeth Roemer on the dangers of emotional avoidance.

   The science of priming is hotly debated. But the main idea here is that by facing failure, it can become easier to manage.

22. John Steinbeck, *East of Eden* (New York: The Viking Press, New York: Penguin Classics, 1952, 2016), 583.

23. Second Corinthians 10:10; 11:6; 25; 12:7; Galatians 4:13–15; Acts 14:19.

24. Second Corinthians 12:10.

25. First Corinthians 15:10 KJV. Formatting mine.

26. Second Corinthians 12:9a. Formatting mine.

CHAPTER 4

1. Raymond Chandler, *The Big Sleep* (New York: Vintage Books, 1939, 1992), 5.

2. Brené Brown, *Rising Strong: How the Ability to Reset Transforms the Way We Live, Love, Parent, and Lead* (New York: Spiegel & Grau, 2015), 129.

3. Mitch Hedberg, "Comedy Central Presents," directed by Paul Miller (Comedy Central, Rickmill Productions, aired January 5, 1999).

4. Henry Cloud and John Townsend, *Boundaries: When To Say Yes, How to Say No* (Grand Rapids, MI: Zondervan, 1992, 2017), 52–53. Emphasis and formatting mine.

5. Solomon Eliot Asch, "Effects of Group Pressure upon the Modification and Distortion of Judgment," in H. Guetzkow (ed.) *Groups, Leadership and Men* (Pittsburgh: Carnegie Press, 1951), 177–90.

6. Julie Exline, Anne Zell, Ellen Bratslavsky, Michelle Hamilton, Anne Swenson, "People-Pleasing Through Eating: Sociotropy Predicts Greater Eating in Response to Perceived Social Pressure," *Journal of Social and Clinical Psychology* 31, no. 2 (February 2012): 169–93.

7. Youjae Yi, Jacob Lee, and Saetbyeol Kim, "Altruistic Indulgence: People Voluntarily Consume High-calorie Foods to Make Other People Feel Comfortable and Pleasant," *Social Influence* 13, no. 4 (November 2018): 223–39.

8. John Powell, *Why Am I Afraid to Tell You Who I Am?* (Great Britain: Fount Paperbacks, 1969, 1999), 4. Formatting mine.

9. Mark Leary, "Sociometer Theory and the Pursuit of Relational Value: Getting to the Root of Self-Esteem," *European Review of Social Psychology* 16 (January 2005): 75–111.

10. Deborah A. O'Helio and Margaret M. Hopkins, "The Impact of Gendered Organizational Systems on Women's Career Advancement," *Frontiers in Psychology* 6, no. 905 (June 2015).

11. Robert W. Livingston and Nicholas A. Pearce, "The Teddy-Bear Effect: Does Having a Baby Face Benefit Black Chief Executive Officers?" *Psychological Science* 20, no. 10 (October 2009): 1229–36.

12. See Alice Miller's *Banished Knowledge* and *For Your Own Good.* Her views are extreme, but her insight is undeniable. She writes, "The only possible recourse a baby has when his screams are ignored is to repress his distress, which is tantamount to mutilating his soul, for the result is an interference with his ability to feel, to be aware, and to remember." *Banished Knowledge: Facing Childhood Injuries* (New York: Anchor Books, 1988, 1991), 2.

13. There are conflicting studies about how to properly "vent" your emotions. Some studies conclude that venting can be physically unhealthy and tends to increase resentment. Others conclude that *expressive journaling,* such as writing about emotions in narrative form, is helpful in regulating emotional distress, especially coupled with self-awareness and self-compassion. Most literature appears to agree that suppressing anger is not a helpful option.

14. "Anger tells us that our boundaries have been violated . . . This is why individuals with injured boundaries often are shocked by the rage they feel inside when they begin setting limits. This is generally not 'new anger'—it's 'old anger.' It's often years of nos that were never voiced, never respected, and never listened to. The protests against all the evil and violation of our souls sit inside us, waiting to tell their truths." Henry Cloud and John Townsend, *Boundaries: When To Say Yes, How to Say No,* 116–117.

15. Psalm 118:6b–7a.

16. Ethan Kross, Emma Bruehlman-Senecal, Jiyoung Park, Aleah Burson, Adrienne Dougherty, Holly Shablack, Ryan Bremner, Jason Moser, Ozlem Ayduk, "Self-Talk as a Regulatory Mechanism: How You Do It Matters," *Journal of Personality and Social Psychology* 106, no. 2 (February 2014): 304–24.

CHAPTER 5

1. Raymond Chandler, *The Long Goodbye* (New York: Vintage Books, 1953, 1992), 3–4.

2. Martin Buber, *I and Thou* (New York: Scribner, 1923, 1970), 110–112.

3. This is similar to Karpman's drama triangle, a social model depicting the Rescuer, the Victim, and the Persecutor. It was popularized in 1968 by Dr. Stephen Karpman. "Fairy Tales and Script Drama Analysis," *Transactional Analysis Bulletin* 7, no. 26, 39–43.

4. Brené Brown, *Rising Strong: How the Ability to Reset Transforms the Way We Live, Love, Parent, and Lead* (New York: Spiegel & Grau, 2015), 78ff.

5. Raymond Chandler, *The Long Goodbye* (New York: Vintage Books, 1953, 1992), 45.

6. Some research shows that hate groups are motivated by complex mythologies, the need to belong, "mission" language, and "defending" against perceived threats.

    Jack Levin, Ashley Reichelmann, "From Thrill to Defensive Motivation: The Role of Group Threat in the Changing Nature of Hate-Motivated Assaults," *American Behavioral Scientist* 59, no. 12 (June 2015): 1546–1561.

7. Guy Raz, "Megan Phelps-Roper: If You're Raised to Hate, Can You Reverse It?" Interview with Megan Phelps-Roper, TED Radio Hour, NPR, Oct. 27, 2017.

8. Leah Remini, *Troublemaker: Surviving Hollywood and Scientology* (New York: Ballantine Books, 2015), 16.

9. Josh Bloch, "Uncover: Escaping NXIVM", Interview with Sarah Edmonson, CBC Podcasts, first aired Sep. 4, 2018.

10. Interview with Josh Riebock by telephone on March 18, 2018.

11. Brené Brown, *Daring Greatly: How the Courage to Be Vulnerable Transforms the Way We Live, Love, Parent, and Lead* (New York: Penguin, 2012, 2015), 99.

12. Sandra L. Murray, John G. Holmes, Dan Dolderman, and Dale W. Griffin, "What the Motivated Mind Sees: Comparing Friends' Perspectives to Married Partners' Views of Each Other," *Journal of Experimental Social Psychology* 36, no. 6 (November 2000): 600–620.

    A study with 105 couples who had been together an average of 10.9 years "revealed that intimates in satisfying marriages perceive more virtue in their partners than their friends or their partners themselves perceive. They also possess partners who see them in this benevolently distorted light. In contrast, intimates in less satisfying marriages perceive less virtue in their partners than their friends or their partners themselves perceive."

    I also recommend the work of John Gottman and Nan Silver. They predicted when marriages would end in divorce with 91% accuracy. Their "four horsemen" of doomed marriages were noted to be criticism, contempt, defensiveness, and stonewalling.

    The Seven Principles for Making Marriage Work: A Practical Guide from the Country's Foremost Relationship Expert (New York: Harmony Books, 1999, 2015), 2, 32–39.

13. John Koenig, *The Dictionary of Obscure Sorrows*, from YouTube channel and blog, http://www.dictionaryofobscuresorrows.com/post/23536922667/sonder.

14. John R. Chambers and Mark H. Davis, "The Role of the Self in Perspective-Taking and Empathy: Ease of Self-Simulation as a Heuristic for Inferring Empathic Feelings," *Social Cognition* 30, no. 2 (April 2012): 153–180.

15. This letter has appeared in many places, the earliest of which appears to be in *Slaying the Giants in Your Life* by David Jeremiah (Nashville: Thomas Nelson, 2001), 68.

16. Matthew 7:1–5, Luke 6:41–42.

CHAPTER 6

1. Donna Tartt, *The Goldfinch* (New York: Little, Brown, and Company, 2013), 8.

2. For research on walking the tightrope between our shortcomings and self-acceptance, see the work of Kristin Neff, Sheila Heen, and Tasha Eurich.

3. The term *malheur* was used this way by French philosopher and activist Simone Weil in her essay "The Love of God and Affliction," from *Waiting for God* (New York: HarperPerennial, 1951, 2009), 67–82.

4. C. S. Lewis, *The Weight of Glory* (1949; repr., New York: HarperCollins, 2001), 170.

5. Charles Haddon Spurgeon, *The Metropolitan Tabernacle Pulpit: Sermons Preached and Revised by C.H. Spurgeon During the Year 1870. Vol. XVI* (London: Passmore and Alabaster, 1871), 448. Sermon "Ripe Fruit" delivered on August 14, 1870.

6. Ephesians 1:4, 7–8a.

CHAPTER 7

1. *The Big Heat*, directed by Fritz Lang, screenplay by Sydney Boehm and William P. McGivern (Culver City, CA: Columbia Pictures, 1953).

2. *Key Largo*, directed by John Huston, screenplay by Richard Brooks and John Huston (Burbank, CA: Warner Bros., 1948). Formatting mine.

3. The original study on ACE Scores was conducted in two parts at Kaiser Permanente with 17,337 participants and published in 1998. Multiple studies have been conducted since. Vincent Felitti, Robert Anda, Dale Nordenberg, David Williamson, Alison Spitz, Valerie Edwards, Mary Koss, James Marks," Relationship of Childhood Abuse and Household Dysfunction to Many of the Leading Causes of Death in Adults: The Adverse Childhood Experiences (ACE) Study," *American Journal of Preventive Medicine* 14, no. 4, (May 1998): 245–58. Also visit: Adverse Childhood Experiences (ACEs), Center for Disease and Control Prevention, https://www.cdc.gov/violenceprevention/acestudy.

4. The original questionnaire can be found in the ACE study published in 1998.
   A version of the ACE test can be found in the appendix of *The Deepest Well*, by Dr. Nadine Harris. Updated tests are still under development. Nadine Burke Harris, *The Deepest Well: Healing the Long-Term Effects of Childhood Adversity* (New York: Houghton Mifflin Harcourt, 2018), 228.

5. Shaoyong Su, Marcia P. Jimenez, Cole T. F. Roberts, and Eric B. Loucks, "The Role of Adverse Childhood Experiences in Cardiovascular Disease Risk: A Review with Emphasis on Plausible Mechanisms," *Current Cardiology Reports* 17, no. 10, art. 88 (October 2015).

6. "[Trauma] can trigger chronic inflammation and hormonal changes that can last a lifetime … and it can dramatically increase the risk for heart disease, stroke, cancer, diabetes—even Alzheimer's … [A] person with four or more ACEs was *twice* as likely to develop heart disease and cancer and *three and a half* times as likely to develop chronic obstructive pulmonary disease (COPD) as a person with zero ACEs … regardless of income or race or access to care … A person with four or more ACEs is two and a half times as likely to smoke, five and a half times as likely to be dependent on alcohol, and ten times as likely to use intravenous drugs as a person with zero ACEs." Nadine Burke Harris, *The Deepest Well: Healing the Long-Term Effects of Childhood Adversity* (New York: Houghton Mifflin Harcourt, 2018), xvii, 38–39, 70.

7. "More than half of those with ACE scores of four or higher reported having learning or behavioral problems … [The] impact of trauma pervaded these patients' adult lives. For example, high ACE scores turned out to correlate with higher workplace absenteeism, financial problems, and lower lifetime income." Bessel van der Kolk, *The Body Keeps the Score: Brain, Mind, and Body in the Healing of Trauma* (New York: Penguin Books, 2014), 145–47.

8. Ibid., 96.

9. Yuichi Shoda, Walter Mischel, Philip K. Peake, "Predicting Adolescent Cognitive and Self-Regulatory Competencies from Preschool Delay of Gratification: Identifying Diagnostic Conditions," *Developmental Psychology* 26, no. 6 (May 1990): 978–86.

10. Tyler W. Watts, Greg J. Duncan, Haonan Quan, "Revisiting the Marshmallow Test: A Conceptual Replication Investigating Links Between Early Delay of Gratification and Later Outcomes," *Psychological Science* 29, no. 7 (May 2018): 1159–77.

11. C. S. Lewis, *Mere Christianity* (New York: HarperCollins 1952, 2001), 91–92.

12. I recognize I have now broken Godwin's Law. I hope you will forgive me this one instance.

13. Rachel Yehuda, Amy Lehrner, "Intergenerational Transmission of Trauma Effects: Putative Role of Epigenetic Mechanisms," *World Psychiatry* 17, no. 3 (October 2018): 243–57.

14. "Can trauma be passed to next generation through DNA?" *PBS News Hour Extra, Daily Video.* Aug. 13, 2015 https://www.pbs.org/newshour/extra/daily-videos/can-trauma-be-passed-to-next-generation-through-dna.

15. Bessel van der Kolk, *The Body Keeps the Score* (New York: Penguin Books, 2014), 68.

16. This phrase was most likely coined by psychiatrist and trauma specialist Dr. Sandra Bloom as early as 1995, who attributed it to social worker and colleague Joseph Foderaro as early as 1991.

17. A clear note here that I can't prescribe anything, but only make suggestions. See the following footnotes for some of the research behind these suggestions. Please also note that it's not enough to "make healthier choices." A study suggests that the discussion around trauma needs to include understanding and changing wider social factors such as intergenerational cycles of poverty. Marilyn Metzler, Melissa T. Merrick, Joanne Klevens, Katie A. Ports, Derek C. Ford, "Adverse Childhood Experiences and Life Opportunities: Shifting the Narrative," *Children and Youth Services Review* 72 (January 2017): 141–49.

18. Mark S. Burton, Andrew A. Cooper, Norah C. Feeny, and Lori A. Zoellner, "The Enhancement of Natural Resilience in Trauma Interventions," *Journal of Contemporary Psychotherapy* 45, no. 4 (December 2015): 193–204.

19. If disclosure isn't the right fit for you, there are alternative therapies that do not require talking such as ART (Accelerated Resolution Therapy) and EMDR (Eye Movement Desensitization and Reprocessing). There are also benefits from "expressive writing." Scott R. Vrana, Rose S. Bono, Andrea Konig, Gabriella C. Scalzo, "Assessing the Coherence of Narratives of Traumatic Events with Latent Semantic Analysis," *Psychological Trauma: Theory, Research, Practice, and Policy* 11, no. 5 (July 2019): 521–24.

20. Mark A. Bellis, Katie Hardcastle, Kat Ford, Karen Hughes, Kathryn Ashton, Zara Quigg, and Nadia Butler, "Does Continuous Trusted Adult Support in Childhood Impart Life-Course Resilience Against Adverse Childhood Experiences - a Retrospective Study on Adult Health-Harming Behaviours and Mental Well-Being," *BMC Psychiatry* 17, no. 1 (March 2017): 110.

21. Christina Bethell, Jennifer Jones, Narangerel Gombojav, Jeff Linkenbach, Robert Sege, "Positive Childhood Experiences and Adult Mental and Relational Health in a Statewide Sample: Associations Across Adverse Childhood Experiences Levels," *JAMA Pediatrics* (September 2019).

22. Bessel van der Kolk, *The Body Keeps the Score*, 330.

23. Nicole J. Hegberg, Jasmeet P. Hayes, and Scott M. Hayes, "Exercise Intervention in PTSD: A Narrative Review and Rationale for Implementation," *Frontiers in Psychiatry* 10, art. 133 (March 2019).

24. Cynthia J. Price and Carole Hooven, "Interoceptive Awareness Skills for Emotion Regulation: Theory and Approach of Mindful Awareness in Body-Oriented Therapy (MABT)," *Frontiers in Psychology* 9, art. 798 (May 2018).

25. Aleksandra Luszczynska, Charles C. Benight, Roman Cieslak, "Self-Efficacy and Health-Related Outcomes of Collective Trauma: A Systematic Review," *European Psychologist* 14, no. 1 (February 2009): 51–62.

26. Adriana Feder, Samoon Ahmad, Elisa J. Lee, Julia E. Morgan, Ritika Singh, Bruce W. Smith, Steven M. Southwick, Dennis S. Charney, "Coping and PTSD Symptoms in Pakistani Earthquake Survivors: Purpose in Life, Religious Coping and Social Support," *Journal of Affective Disorders* 147, no. 1–3 (May 2013): 156–63.

   Tanya N. Alim, Adriana Feder, Ruth Elaine Graves, Yanping Wang, James Weaver, Maren Westphal, Angelique Alonso, Notalelomwan U. Aigbogun, Bruce W. Smith, John T. Doucette, Thomas A. Mellman, William B. Lawson, Dennis S. Charney, "Trauma, Resilience, and Recovery in a High-Risk African-American Population," *The American Journal of Psychiatry* 165, no. 12 (December 2008): 1566–75.

27. Kelli Nicole Triplett, Richard Glenn Tedeschi, Arnie Cann, Lawrence G. Calhoun, and Charlie L. Reeve, "Posttraumatic Growth, Meaning in Life, and Life Satisfaction in Response to Trauma," *Psychological Trauma: Theory, Research, Practice, and Policy* 4, no. 4 (June 2012): 400–410.

28. Second Corinthians 5:17. Formatting mine.

CHAPTER 8

1. *Interstellar*, directed by Christopher Nolan, screenplay by Jonathan and Christopher Nolan (Los Angeles: Paramount Pictures; Burbank, CA: Warner Bros., 2014).

2. See the work of psychologist Murray Bowen and his Eight Concepts of Family Systems Theory. https://thebowencenter.org/theory/eight-concepts.

3. The overfunctioner/underfunctioner paradigm was first coined by Murray Bowen circa 1978 and later popularized in Harriet Lerner's *The Dance of Anger: A Woman's Guide to Changing the Patterns of Intimate Relationships* (New York: HarperCollins, 1985, 2014), 21 and chapter 7, 121–53.

4. Murray Bowen, *Family Therapy in Clinical Practice* (Lanham, MD: Rowman & Littlefield Publishers, 1985, 2004), 472–75.

5. Ibid., 473.

CHAPTER 9

1. Tim O'Brien, *The Things They Carried* (New York: Houghton Mifflin, 1990, 2009), 226.

2. Kate Bowler, *Everything Happens for a Reason: And Other Lies I've Loved* (New York: Random House, 2018), 70. Formatting mine.

3. In Mexico, there are shrines with rows of pictures and candles and heirlooms, on set days and sites, to commemorate generations of ancestors. Scripture has entire pages of celebrated names. In the Hindu tradition, ashes of the deceased are often spread over the sacred waters of the Ganges. The Toraja, an indigenous group in Indonesia, have a funeral ceremony that is weeks or even years long; the family members chat with the body, continue to have dinner together, and every August the body is exhumed, cleaned, and put in new clothes. And to be fair, in the 1800s, the invention of photography began a trend in America and Europe in which families posed for photos with their deceased loved ones. The trend ceased in the 1930s when death became more medicalized. For more, check out *From Here to Eternity: Traveling the World to Find the Good Death* (New York: W. W. Norton & Company, 2018) by Caitlin Doughty.

4. J. D. Salinger, *The Catcher in the Rye* (Boston: Little, Brown and Company, 1945, 2001), 158.

5. Martha W. Hickman, *Healing After Loss: Daily Meditations for Working Through Grief* (New York: HarperCollins, 1994), 170.
6. C. S. Lewis, *Till We Have Faces: A Myth Retold* (New York: HarperOne, 1956, 2017), 345.
7. Revelation 21:4 KJV. Formatting mine.
8. Tim O'Brien, *The Things They Carried*, 213.

CHAPTER 10

1. Simon Tugwell, *Ways of Imperfection: An Explanation of Christian Spirituality* (Springfield, IL: Templegate, 1985), 87. The phrase "Pay attention to yourself" was said frequently in early Christian ascetic circles. It's perhaps first recorded in the fourth century writings of Father Isaiah, in the 27th of his 29 letters called the Ascetic Discourses. It was also said in a letter from John the Prophet to Barsanuphius the Great in the sixth century, as translated by John Chryssavgis in *The Fathers of the Church* (Washington, D.C.: The Catholic University of America Press, 2007) 19, 88, and various pages.
2. Raymond Chandler, *Farewell, My Lovely* (New York: Vintage Books, 1940, 1992), 25.
3. This is, in fact, the title of Timothy Wilson's book *Strangers to Ourselves: Discovering the Adaptive Unconscious* (Boston: Harvard University Press, 2002).
4. The view I'm presenting here is simplified. The automatic self is partially what psychologist Carl Jung refers to as the "shadow." It can be summed up by Jonathan Miller: "Human beings owe a surprisingly large proportion of their cognitive and behavioral capacities to the existence of an 'automatic self' of which they have no conscious knowledge and over which they have little voluntary control." Jonathan Miller, "Going Unconscious," *New York Review of Books*, April 20, 1995, 65. Also reprinted in *Hidden Histories of Science* (New York: New York Review Books, 1995), 27–28. Psychologist Jonathan Haidt offered a helpful analogy called "the elephant rider," in which the rider is our "conscious reasoning—the stream of words and images of which we are fully aware," but the elephant "is the other 99 percent of mental processes—the ones that occur outside of awareness but that actually govern most of our behavior." Jonathan Haidt, *The Righteous Mind: Why Good People Are Divided by Politics and Religion* (New York: Vintage Books, 2012, 2013), xxi, 52–60. Functionally speaking, the conscious self is often discussed as an "operating attention" to the task at hand, while the automatic self is the "autopilot" that turns the task into a habit. The first time you drive to a new place, the conscious self is attentive to all the surroundings, but the more you drive to that place, the more the automatic self will take over until you can drive with little thought. In functional cases, like driving, the conscious and automatic selves are neutral and cooperative. In philosophical and social cases, like stereotyping and group dynamics, the two selves are often in conflict.
5. Of course, you need an automatic self. Your brain needs to take shortcuts in order to make fast decisions. That's how humans survived so long; our brains and bodies found ways to use the least amount of calories for the most amount of response. The problem is that we're still using very little cognitive resources for some of our deepest, most underlying beliefs.

Hans Rosling, *Factfulness: Ten Reasons We're Wrong About the World—and Why Things Are Better Than You Think* (New York: Flatiron Books, 2018), 15. Psychologist Daniel Kahneman also popularized the idea of two types of thinking: System 1, which is faster but often leads to wrong judgments, and System 2, which is slower but yields more accurate conclusions. For clear decision-making, we need both systems: "Constantly questioning our own thinking would be impossibly tedious, and System 2 is much too slow and inefficient to serve as a substitute for System 1 in making routine decisions. The best we can do is a compromise: learn to recognize situations in which mistakes are likely and try harder to avoid significant mistakes when the stakes are high." Daniel Kahneman, *Thinking, Fast and Slow* (New York: Farrar, Straus and Giroux, 2011), 28.

6. Lauren A. Leotti, Sheena S. Iyengar, and Kevin N. Ochsner, "Born to Choose: The Origins and Value of the Need for Control," *Trends in Cognitive Sciences* 14, no. 10 (October 2010): 457–63.

7. Joachim C. Brunstein, "Implicit Motives and Explicit Goals: The Role of Motivational Congruence in Emotional Well-Being," in *Implicit Motives*, ed. Oliver C. Schultheiss and Joachim C. Brunstein (New York: Oxford University Press, 2010), 358–59.

   Excerpt: "across Western and nonWestern cultures, Hofer and colleagues consistently found that the alignment of implicit motives on the one hand and explicit values and life goals on the other hand was associated with enhanced well-being whereas discrepancies between implicit motives and explicit goals were negatively related to well-being."

8. Yuval Noah Harari, *Sapiens: A Brief History of Humankind* (New York: HarperCollins, 2015), 114.

9. Ibid.

10. Anaïs Nin, *Seduction of the Minotaur* (Athens, OH: Swallow Press, 1961, 1969), 124. Formatting mine.

11. For in-group and out-group dynamics, see the Robbers Cave experiment conducted in 1954 or the Stanford Prison experiment conducted in 1971.

12. Some studies suggest that "extreme partisanship," or heightened loyalty to an in-group, is addictive.

13. One of the pioneering explorations into confirmation bias is from this study: Raymond Nickerson, "Confirmation Bias: A Ubiquitous Phenomenon in Many Guises," *Review of General Psychology* 2, no. 2 (June 1998): 175–220.

14. Attributed to Lowell L. Bennion, *Religion and the Pursuit of Truth* (Salt Lake City: Deseret Book Co., 1959), 52.

15. In more spiritual circles, discernment can also mean finding our path, knowing "God's will," or figuring out our next step or how to make a decision.

16. I'm paraphrasing a lot, but this was essentially the entire crux of the sermon preached by Jake English, circa 2008.

17. First Thessalonians 5:20–22.

18. Acts 17:11 KJV.

19. Psalm 13:3.

20. There's an online training exercise that has been able to successfully "vaccinate" participants from misinformation.

    Jon Roozenbeek and Sander van der Linden, "Fake News Game Confers Psychological Resistance Against Online Misinformation," *Palgrave Communications* 65, no. 1 (June 2019).

21. C. S. Lewis, *The Abolition of Man* (New York: HarperCollins, 1944, 1974), 82. To "see through things for ever" is called infinite regress. It's like a kid continually asking, "Why?"

CHAPTER 11

1. Brenda Ueland, *If You Want to Write: A Book about Art, Independence, and Spirit* (Minneapolis: G. P. Putnam's Sons, Graywolf Press, 1938, 1987, 2007), 4. Formatting mine.

2. Howard Thurman, "The Sound of the Genuine," Baccalaureate Address at Spelman College, May 4, 1980. From *The Spelman Messenger*, vol. 96, no. 4, Summer 1980, 14–15, as edited by Jo Moore Stewart.

3. Ibid.

4. Sascha Topolinski, Sandy Lindner, Anna Freudenberg, "Popcorn in the cinema: Oral interference sabotages advertising effects," *Journal of Consumer Psychology* 24, no. 2 (April 2014): 169–76.

5. Frederick Buechner, *Wishful Thinking: A Theological ABC* (New York: Harper & Row, 1973), 95.

6. C.S. Lewis, *Mere Christianity* (New York: HarperCollins 1952, 2001), 198.

7. For a helpful list of values to examine, see Brené Brown's *Dare to Lead: Brave Work. Tough Conversations. Whole Hearts.* (New York: Random House, 2018), 188. She writes: "We Can't Live into Values That We Can't Name" (187).

8. Ibid., 185.

9. Kathy Khang, *Raise Your Voice: Why We Stay Silent and How to Speak Up* (Downers Grove, IL: InterVarsity Press, 2018), 3.

10. Jeremiah 1:6 KJV.

11. Jeremiah 16:1, 8.

12. Jeremiah 19:9.

13. Jeremiah 20:2; 37:15; 38:6.

14. Jeremiah 25:11; Ezra 1:1.

CHAPTER 12

1. J. D. Salinger, *The Catcher in the Rye* (Boston: Little, Brown and Company, 1945, 2001), 224.

2. From a speech given by Carl Rogers in 1964 called "Experiences in Communication," transcribed in his book *A Way of Being* (New York: Houghton Mifflin, 1980, 1995), 12.

3. Scott Alexander, "The Categories Were Made for Man, Not Man for the Categories," *Slate Star Codex* (blog), November 21, 2014, http://slatestarcodex.com/2014/11/21/the-categories-were-made-for-man-not-man-for-the-categories.

4. Zora Neale Hurston, *Dust Tracks on a Road* (New York: HarperPerennial, 1942, 1996), 176.

5. Barry Lopez, *Crow and Weasel* (New York: North Point Press, 1990), 60.

6. Kerry Egan, *On Living* (New York: Riverhead Books, 2016), 65.

7. Matthew 27:11–26; Mark 15:1–15; John 18:28–40.

8. Luke 23:34.

9. Mark 16:7.

CONCLUSION

1. Revelation 7:9.

2. First John 4:12.

ADULTING GOT YOU DOWN?

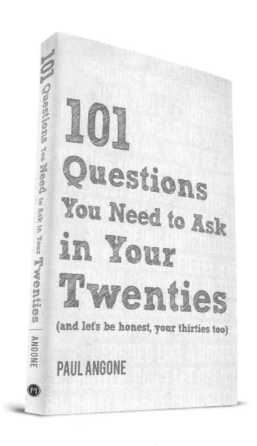

After his success with *101 Secrets for Your Twenties*, Paul Angone captures that same hilarious, accurate assessment of life as a modern-day twentysomething, but now he's digging deeper. It's time to move beyond desperately trying not to fail and take a swing at thriving.

978-0-8024-1691-9 | also available as eBook and audiobook

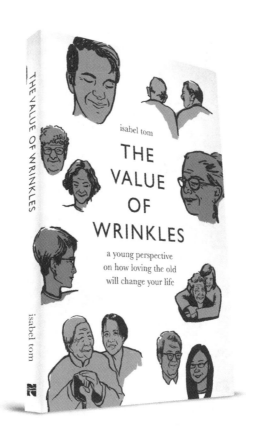